WINDERMERE
WALKING AROUND THE LAKE

WINDERMERE

walking around the lake in easy stages

Duncan Turner

First published in 2006
by Palatine Books,
Carnegie House,
Chatsworth Road
Lancaster LA1 4SL
www.palatinebooks.com

British Library Cataloguing-in-Publication data
A catalogue record for this book is available from the British Library

ISBN 10: 1-874181-34-9
ISBN 13: 978-1-874181-34-7

Typeset by Carnegie Book Production
www.carnegiebookproduction.com
Printed and bound by Cambridge University Press

Contents

Important Information

This walk can be done by the enthusiastic long-distance walker as a complete 30-mile circuit of Lake Windermere in one day, starting and finishing at Ambleside/Waterhead. But for lesser mortals like myself I have broken it down into four, or five, easy stages which can be done at different times. In addition, there are six further, shorter walks which are in the vicinity of the lake. THIS IS NOT A WALK AROUND THE SHORELINE as there are many points where access is not allowed. Rather it describes a route which encircles the lake, sometimes veering as much as a mile away from the shore itself.

Acknowledgements

The writing and production of this book is not entirely my own work; though I have, of course, written the text, taken the photographs and drawn the maps. First I must thank the staff of Carnegie Publishing whose enthusiasm and care is in part responsible for what you see and hold in your hand. I think they have produced a wonderful book. I must also thank my wife, Carole, who has not only accompanied me on many days as I have tramped these paths but has also supported me in my efforts to get it all down on paper. I would also like to thank Mary Higham whose classes on the history and geography of the North West of England I attended after I retired from work. Her enthusiasm, together with her vast and detailed knowledge of all aspects of the subject, is why I started to write this and other books. It is from her that I have learned to see and note things on my walks and later to find out 'why' and 'how' and 'what for'. She has added another dimension to the pleasure I gain from walking in our splendid countryside and I am most grateful to her for all her support. Most importantly I should like to say thank you to all the landowners who have provided 'permissive paths' across their land. Without this permission *Walking Around the Lake* would not be half as enjoyable.

My brother, Alan, has spent much time checking the route for errors and omissions, not to mention grammar and spellings. Also he and Bill Pickering, who helped verify my first book, have checked out most of the script with the route on the ground, and my thanks go to them. Nothing is perfect, of course, and despite the efforts of Alan and Bill there will be an occasional error but hopefully nothing too catastrophic. At the time of going to press the details of the route were accurate but things do change, buildings are put up or taken down, barns become houses for instance, or paths are sometimes altered and stiles become gates. So when you use this book do not be surprised if a stile has become a kissing gate and the path goes in a rather different direction than detailed. What will not change so dramatically is the landscape, though it will gradually change.

Proceeds of the Book

During the course of *Windermere: Walking around the Lake* you will pass Holehird. Details of the house and garden are given within the text and mention is made of the house where severely disabled people live with much loving care and assistance.

For more than 40 years the house has been used for this purpose by the Leonard Cheshire organisation, but in 2003 they decided that it was no longer suitable for their purposes and so resolved to close their activities here and move to a new, purpose built house at Garstang, just north of Preston. At the time of writing, March 2006, plans are still not finalised and they are likely to remain at Holehird for a further two years.

There have always been many local volunteers assisting the staff at Holehird and naturally they have become firm friends with those who live there. The house was originally donated in 1945 by its last owner, Alderman Groves, for the benefit of the community, preferably to be used in the care of the sick and infirm In the sure knowledge that many of those residents do not wish to move, a group of local volunteers are endeavouring to ensure that the residents remain in the house with the help of the new Holehird charity. They need to raise £1.5 million pounds to start it up and a lot of money thereafter to keep it going.

I'm inspired by the thought that this small body of people have embarked on such a large and worthwhile project, so I have decided that all the funds raised from this book will go to new Holehird. By purchasing this book you will also have made a donation towards the care and support of severely disabled people.

Further donations can be sent to: The Treasurer, New Holehird, c/o Temple Heelis, 41 Crescent Road, Windermere LA23 1BL. You can send as much as you want, no amount too big or small – £1 million to £1. If you are a UK taxpayer you can also 'Gift Aid' it and thereby provide another 28 pence in the pound. (At the time of going to press, March 2006). The Treasurer will be pleased to send you a Gift Aid declaration form Registered Charity No: 1102609.

Introduction

I should like to make it clear this walk does not follow the shore of Windermere since much of the shoreline is in private ownership, particularly on the eastern side, not to mention the almost total lack of footpaths alongside the lake. What I have done is to detail a route on footpaths, bridleways and roads encircling the lake; some of which are as much as a mile (1.6 km) away from the lake shore. For much of the route the lake is visible, but on the eastern sector you will be out of sight of the lake quite regularly.

If it were possible to follow the shoreline the walk would be approximately 27½ miles (44 km) in length and my route is 30 miles (48 km), which isn't a lot further. The shoreline has many inlets, bays and promontories whereas my route, although apparently much further when looking at a map, is actually more direct and straight-forward and that is why it is only three miles longer than the shoreline. The western route, between Lakeside and Waterhead, follows the shoreline quite closely in three separate stretches: ¾ mile (1.2 km), 1¼ miles (2 km) and 3¾ miles (6 km), but sadly the eastern route doesn't take you anywhere near the water, except at Fell Foot. It's true there are some very short stretches of paths along the eastern shore side of the lake. These are found at Waterhead, Miller Ground, Bowness and Fell Foot, but walking these shoreline paths would only make the route tedious since a rather big detour would have to be made to walk along them. The total ascent for the circular walk is 4707 ft (1435m), almost the equivalent of climbing up Scafell Pike 1½ times! The longest and highest ascent is 580 ft (177m) over a distance of 3 miles (4.8 km), which is reasonably gentle.

Despite being unable to stroll alongside the eastern shoreline the route ascends in several places to provide memorable views of the lake. These viewpoints also provide the opportunity of espying many of the surrounding Lakeland fells, as well as several excellent panoramas of the Howgills and the Pennines to the east, Bowland Forest to the south-east and Morecambe Bay to the south. You will understand that fine weather cannot be guaranteed and that these views can only be enjoyed when the climatic conditions are favourable; particularly in winter on a cold and crisp, sunny day.

I suggest the route be completed in four easy stages, as detailed in the book, with the option of doing it in five stages. However, if you are very fit and an enthusiastic long-distance walker no doubt you will rise to the challenge and complete the whole round in one day. Walking at an average speed of 3 miles per hour, without stops, you will easily do it in 10 hours! It should be noted that 2 miles an hour is a more realistic speed for the average walker. All the times I quote ignore the fact you may stop numerous times *en route*.

The distances and heights are given in both imperial (British) and metric measures, since I am aware that many who use this book will not be totally at ease with our splendid system of measurement. You may already know all the details but in simple terms: 1 mile = 1.6 km and 1 yard is just about 3 cms shorter than 1 metre, therefore when I mention yards I don't bother to convert to metres since there isn't a lot of difference. There are 3 feet in 1 yard, so 1 foot is about 32 cms; which is the same length as my feet, so you understand why I find our system so simple!

The book has been written assuming that you will walk around the circuit in a clockwise manner, and the main text details this route. As I have said above, the whole circular walk is 30 miles (48 km). If you split the walk into two sectors – Ambleside to Fell Foot, which is 16¼ miles (26 km), and then the 13¾ miles (22 km) from Lakeside to Ambleside – you will have two very good day walks. An anti-clockwise route is also detailed more briefly.

For the benefit of the casual walker the walk also conveniently splits into four, or five, relatively easy stages and, including the exit and entry routes, the distances for each stage are: Ambleside to Bowness, 10 miles/16 km, Bowness to Fellfoot, 8¾ miles/14 km, Lakeside to Ferry House and across the lake to Bowness (plus the ride on the ferry), 7½ miles/12 km. Then from Bowness to Ferry Nab, across the lake by car ferry and on to Ambleside, 7¾ miles/12.5 km. Waterhead to Lindeth Lane at 10 miles may be a bit too far for some, so I've suggested this can be spilt into two shorter stages: Waterhead to Windermere town 5¼ miles, and Windermere to Bowness 4½ miles. When you add routes to and from Bowness to join up with the route proper the total is 34 miles (54.5 km). The other parts can be shortened but I don't describe how since the logistics of getting back to your starting point are a somewhat complex. So you will have to make your own decision on this.

It's convenient that you can catch the steamer or a launch back from Lakeside to Bowness and/or Ambleside-Waterhead and vice versa in the summer months, usually from Easter to the end of October. During this time a little ferry operated by the National Trust also runs between Fell Foot and Lakeside, though walkers will have to keep an eye on the time to fit in with the schedule. A not-so-regular bus runs along the eastern side of Windermere and during the winter this is what you will probably have to use, rather than a launch or steamer. Public transport is not readily available on the western shore. Whatever you choose, do check times before you set off.

The travel arrangements aren't easy on the other stages either. Anyhow, these are all merely suggestions and I'm sure you will work out your own itinerary. It's just a matter of the logistics of getting to the start and then back again which is the real problem. The obvious answer is to have a friend or spouse who doesn't walk and who will deliver you to the starting point by car and collect you at the end of the day; a much easier operation now we all seem to have mobile phones! However, to save road congestion, I would always encourage the use of public transport where possible. The more it's used, the more it's likely to stay and possibly become cheaper.

I have given approximate walking times for each stage but you must understand that these are just a guide and are based on walking at 2 miles per hour (3.2 km per hour). The times given do not include any stoppages and these could easily add one hour or more to your walk.

Public Transport Information

Whilst on the subject of transport here are a few tips about the use of buses and boats. It's best if you go to a tourist information centre to get up-to-date timetables before you set off on your walk. Sadly I can't print them here since they change from year-to-year and even from season-to-season, so I hope you will understand. However, you may find these telephone numbers and websites useful:

Buses: Stagecoach in Cumbria – Services 599, 555/556 and 618, phone: 08706082 608
Windermere Steamboat Company – phone: 015395 31188 or www.windermere-lakecruises.co.uk

These two companies offer combined tickets and so it's worth asking for details of these.

If you are walking in the summer months, between Easter and the end of October, you will find it easier to use public transport than during the winter months, November to April. This is especially the case with the steamers and launches, though the Windermere Car Ferry does operate throughout the year.

Maps and Points of Interest

I've assumed the starting point as Ambleside-Waterhead. This is arbitrary and you can, in fact, start anywhere on the route and I'm sure many people will do so.

You should be able to follow my route on the 1:25000 scale Ordnance Survey Map: *Explorer OL 7, The English Lakes South Eastern Area.* The smaller scale Landranger Maps 90 *Penrith & Keswick* and *90 Kendal & Morecambe* 1:50000 versions will also suffice but I never use these since I find them too small a scale to provide the detail I require. These smaller scale maps are, however, useful when trying to work out the names of the distant fells. At the time of writing, 2006, the titles of maps have recently changed. *Explorer OL7* used to be known as *Outdoor Leisure 7* and the cover was yellow. The cover of the current one is tangerine and clearly shows 'access land'. By the time you come to do this walk it is possible Ordnance Survey will have re-numbered and re-designed it yet again.

I have also provided a number of options within the walks directions. These give alternative routes to miss out parts of the walk that involve ascents, providing you with a low level alternative. I have included various notes on points of interest *en route*; at least they interest me and so I suppose they may interest you! If not, just skip over the numbered paragraphs in italics.

Should you decide to undertake the walk anti-clockwise, and I'm sure many people will do this, it will make following the 'information notes' a little more difficult, since my notes may refer to the 'barn on your left' which will, of course, be on your 'right' but I'm sure you will be able to cope with this anomaly.

To the best of my knowledge the given information is accurate. However, I'm well aware that some who read this book will be more knowledgeable than me and able to find fault with some of my information. In anticipation of that, please accept my humble apologies

What to wear and carry with you

What you wear and carry with you is entirely your own choice, of course, but I can assure you that you will not pass anywhere to eat or get a drink on the route, so you will have to carry these with you. Whatever you decide don't forget to carry some water, at least 1 litre. There aren't any toilet facilities *en route* either, but there are numerous bushes and trees and many, many walls for you to seek comfort and privacy. Please bury used tissues.

Whilst on the subject of comfort I always feel that if you are wearing a good pair of walking shoes or boots you will end the day in relative comfort. Almost the entire route is on good paths, tracks and roads but there are also a few sections where there will be mud and water after rain – most of the year! The most important thing about footwear is the sole; it should be thick and have a good tread. I have seen far too many people wearing trainers and Wellington boots who have developed blisters. These are just not suitable footwear for a long walk. Most of the use of my first aid kit over the years has been in the care of the feet of others who were inappropriately shod, so be warned. The sun does sometimes shine, so as well as wet weather gear have a suitable hat to keep off the worst of the sun, and sun cream is another must in my kit, even in winter. The route is, of course, undulating but none of the ascents is very long, though one or two are steep in short stretches. This applies to descents as well. If you have a walking pole, or poles, I'm sure you will find them useful.

The Countryside Code

You may have heard of The Countryside Code but not exactly know what it is. To quote from a leaflet, a simple summary of it is this:

From a gentle stroll or relaxing picnic to a long-distance walk or heart-pumping adventure, the countryside provides every opportunity for enjoyment and relaxation.

BE SAFE AND PLAN AHEAD

LEAVE GATES AND PROPERTY AS YOU FIND THEM

PROTECT PLANTS AND ANIMALS AND TAKE YOUR LITTER HOME

KEEP DOGS UNDER CLOSE CONTROL

CONSIDER OTHER PEOPLE

From 1 March–31 July you must keep your dog on a short lead.

Sensible and easy to understand, I'm sure you will agree.

Windermere – facts and figures

First of all, the name of the lake. It was first documented in the twelfth century as *Wonwaldremere*, *Winendemere*, *Wynandrem* and *Winandermer*, all meaning 'Lake of a man called Vinandar'; a mixture of Old Norse *Vinandr* plus the Old English *mere*. There are other theories but this is the most popular one, supported by eminent place-name experts. The length of the lake is 11¼ miles or 18.08 km At its widest point, between the Low Wood Hotel and Pull Wyke inlet, it is 1 mile and 520 yards wide, though the usually quoted widest part of the lake is between Miller Ground and Belle Grange, at 1540 yards wide. Its deepest point is between the Lake District Visitor Centre at Brockhole and High Wray Bay where the bottom of the lake is 219 ft (67m) below the surface. I'm sorry but I can't tell you exactly how many gallons of water the lake holds but have read that there are 320,000,000,000 litres on average. If like me you find all those noughts meaningless I believe it means 320 billion. You'll have to ask someone else how many gallons that is but I think it's around 70 billion! It is without doubt the longest, biggest natural lake in England and when you've completed the circuit you can tell people what you've done and in all probability they won't be the slightest bit impressed. However, I'm absolutely sure you will have enjoyed the experience.

The Clockwise Route

The start of the walk at Waterhead, seen from the pierhead.

Waterhead to Lindeth Lane

8¾ miles (13.5 km),
approximately 4 hours 15 minutes
Total ascent 1661 ft (507m)

The start is opposite the pier head at Waterhead, next to the bus stop on the main Ambleside–Windermere road. Across the road and to your right is the Waterhead Hotel and adjacent is the Lake House Hotel. Follow the sign to Jenkin Crag which takes you up a steep, rocky path and over a stile into a pasture. At the far side of the pasture there is a ladder stile over into Skelghyll Woods. The path ascends upwards through the trees, so you ignore a path descending to the right. Eventually it joins another path where you turn right.

To enter from Ambleside

This is about 200 yards further

If you are staying in Ambleside there isn't any need to go to Waterhead. Just walk along the main road (A591) from the middle of Ambleside in the direction of Windermere to Fisherbeck car park, just opposite Hayes Garden Centre. In fact you may wish to leave your car here for about 6 or 7 hours. Walk away from the main road to Skelghyll Lane at the rear. Turn right and follow the lane which soon ascends steeply up hill. Follow the signs to Skelghyll Wood and Jenkin Crag. The path from Waterhead joins this path from the right as you enter the woods.

Soon the track bears left and rises steeply and it's rough underfoot; so tread carefully, especially in wet conditions. Cross over Stencher Beck by the bridge and either take the left-hand bend, a gentler ascent, or carry straight on upwards. After another short, steep stretch of track the path becomes less steep.

(1) *This track used to be the 'drove road' from Ambleside to Troutbeck and from there up the Garburn Road into Kentmere. From there it climbed over into Longsleddale then south down the valley and eventually into the Lune Valley. Up until the middle of the nineteenth century, in fact until the coming of railways, cattle and sheep would be driven along drove roads to the markets in the big cities and towns further south. So use your imagination and you will see hundreds of cattle and up to 2000 sheep being driven along this track by the drovers who would be on foot, not on horseback like the cowboys in the United States.*

Look out on your right-hand side for the silver 'National Trust' sign indicating Jenkin's Crag on your right, over the wall. You will notice this time it has an apostrophe 's'.

The entry to the 'lookout' at Jenkin Crag.

(2) *Sometimes Jenkin Crag is also known as 'Jenkin's Crag', 'Jenkins Crag' or 'Jenkyn's Crag'. You may notice signs with all these spellings but it's the placement of the apostrophes which intrigues me. However, I've used the Ordnance Survey spelling, which is no guarantee that it's the correct one, but at least it's the name which most people will be accustomed to. Jenkin by the way is the local dialect name for John. I'm afraid I don't know*

who Jenkin was, however I think he must have been a farmer, or landowner, since there is a field directly below the crag next to the road between the Low Wood Hotel and Waterhead called 'Jenkin Field'. For all I know he could have been a Welshman, since Jenkin is a popular Welsh surname. Also we mustn't forget that the Welsh are more related to the Ancient British than the English, and that the Ancient British lived here in the Lake District longer than in the rest of England. That's why the old county of Cumberland gained its name; 'the land of the Cumri' and now we have a County of Cumbria. The Welsh for Wales is of course 'Cymru', pronounced 'cumry'.

It's well worth a minute or two to go to the outcrop and look out over Windermere towards Wray on the far shore, the Coniston fells further in the distance and, over to the right, the Langdale Pikes and other central fells.

(3) Take note of the rock here. It is of the 'Borrowdale Volcanic Group', or 'BVG' as it's more commonly known, and it's a good example, I believe, of what is known as 'pyroclastic flow', consisting of lumps (clasts) of rock thrown up from more than one source. It's been worn down by all the boots of those who visit this spot but away from the main viewpoints you can see the clasts more readily.

Returning to the track, turn right and continue the gradual climb upwards until the path is less steep and levels out.

(4) The rock below you is a specific limestone known as Coniston Limestone, a narrow band of siltstone no more than a mile wide which stretches from Millom, on the coast near Barrow to Shap, passing across the northern reaches of Windermere. It overlays the BVG and is on the boundary of that rock and the softer Stockdale Shales of the Silurian period. This is why the topography to the south is gentler and less imposing than the fells to the north. The rocks have worn down more readily than the tougher volcanics. I'm no geologist but have been fascinated to find out about this particular 'unconformity', as I believe it's known, and anyone can see that the landscape is less rugged now.

11

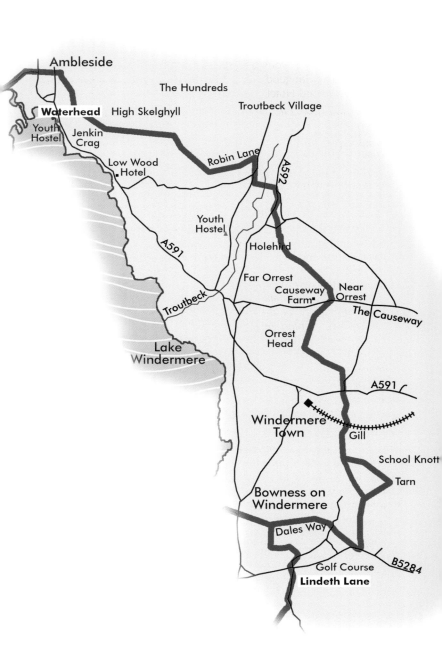

Soon you leave the woods and the track 'contours' round to High Skelghyll Farm, with good views away on your right and down below you the Low Wood Hotel.

(5) I'm not sure of the derivation of Skelghyll but I do know that on Thomas Jeffrys' map of 1770 it is spelled 'Skel Gill' and it would seem that the 'ghyll' spelling has only become common since William Wordsworth started to spell it that way early in the nineteenth century. The Low Wood Hotel is now very highly rated but it was originally a simple inn. In 1844 a meeting was held here to protest about the plans to bring the railway from Windermere to Ambleside, and even on to Keswick over Dunmail Raise. Amongst the local notables present was William Wordsworth, the most well-known personality, having just been appointed Poet Laureate. He wrote two very critical letters, including specially written sonnets to the Morning Post, *later incorporated into the* Daily Telegraph, *which brought the topic into the public domain. His main argument was that it would spoil the nature of the Lake District but I suspect a darker motive was behind his protest. The campaign was won, of course, but later Wordsworth bought shares in the line, despite his complaint that it was bringing common folk to 'assault' his treasured Lake District. Another example of the profound effect the poet had on the Lake District. You pass the hotel on your way by road from Windermere/Bowness to Ambleside; indeed you may even be staying there.*

Soon you cross over a cattle-grid after which you will find a kissing gate on your left. Go through and climb upwards, steeply at first, to the crossing over a beck and then more gradually up to a gate. Here 'Hundreds Road' leads off and upwards to your left and leading to, you will not be surprised to learn, 'The Hundreds' on the south-eastern slopes of Wansfell Pike (826 ft/251m).

(6) A 'hundred' is an old English division of land that was supposed to contain a hundred families. However, I do wonder whether this was actually the case here since it is a very small parcel of land and would never have been big enough to sustain one hundred families. So the name may have a different

Looking down the length of Windermere from Robin Lane.

derivation. Even today I doubt if there are 100 families living in this part of Troutbeck.

Bear right and follow Robin Lane, which gradually descends towards Troutbeck with the slopes of Wansfell up on your left. After a couple of minutes there is a junction with a path leading off down to your right and opposite this is a stile in the wall which leads up to a cairn, marked as 'Pillar' on the Ordnance Survey map.

(7) I've been told this cairn was erected in the eighteenth century by Thomas West as one of his 'Viewing Stations' for those travelling through the Lakes using his Guide to the Lakes, *but I don't think this is correct. I've also been told it's a 'surveying cairn' used in conjunction with the Thirlmere viaduct, though I have to say it's nothing like the two others in the vicinity which are located on the slope of Wansfell just above Skelghyll Woods. They are different in construction and look a lot newer than this one. So take your pick, or perhaps you really do know the answer; in which case perhaps you will let me know!*

A few minutes later another track leads off to the right and a conveniently placed seat here gives you the opportunity to rest a while and enjoy a good view down the lake. About 600 yards further on look for a narrow track off to your right leading steeply down a narrow passage. This soon emerges through a cluster of houses onto the road which winds up through the village of Troutbeck, most of which is spread out along the road for over a mile up to your left However, you turn right and soon you come to Townend, the house on your right and the distinctive barn on your left. The National Trust now owns this old farm and if you feel you have the time it's worthwhile spending an hour here. On the other hand it may be better to plan a visit some other time.

(8) Townend is truly a magnificent example of a seventeenth-century yeoman's house and was occupied by the Browne family from 1626 until 1943. The solid stone and slate house with its distinctive round chimneys is filled with fascinating artefacts typical of a farming household in Lakeland. There are also good examples of authentic furniture and furnishings, which belonged to the Brownes. My favourite is the grand oak table, which must have been built inside the house. When I visited I sat at the table and imagined the conversations that would have taken place around it during all the years the family

Townend, the seventeenth-century yeoman's house inhabited by the Browne family from 1626 to 1943.

The terracing on the pasture on the path just up form the road at Troutbeck.

inhabited the house. The barn opposite is equally interesting and, again, is an outstanding example of a typical 'bank barn' found in the Lake District. Built in 1666 its most interesting feature is that it is set on a slope and the upside entry would be where the corn or hay would be taken into the upper floor and down below would be where the cattle were kept. The spinning gallery on the entry level is also a feature and in most cases these are found to be facing north. There are various theories about this but I won't go into them here.

So, having left or gone past Townend, carry on down the road and take the left-hand fork and descend for about 250 yards until you come to a little gathering of houses, next to which there is a path going sharply up to the right. However, you turn left here, down the track with the house on your left and the garden over the wall on your right. Soon you stride over two footbridges across Trout Beck and then go through the gate and up the track at the other side. This steep but short path leads you out onto the main road up through Troutbeck from Windermere which also goes over Kirkstone Pass into Patterdale and Ullswater. Turn right and walk along the roadside pavement and then the permissive path, which soon emerges onto the roadside path again. After a further 100 yards, with a field gate on your right, cross over and go through the kissing gate opposite. Climb diagonally right up the path through the sloping pasture, cross over the beck and carry on upwards.

(9) As you climb up you may notice the terracing on the steep slopes. Some say this was man made but I asked the farmer about it one day and he reckoned it was just natural landslip caused by the constant grazing of sheep.

At the top you will find another seat, shaded by a large beech tree, which you may want to use for a minute or two whilst you enjoy the view across Windermere and towards the Coniston fells, Bowfell and the Langdale Pikes. Striding on you climb over a stile and pass between a barn and a house. They make wood burning stoves here, if you need one. Cross over the lane and take the track opposite to Far Orrest. Soon there is a track leading down to your right. This goes to Holehird, the house and the gardens, but I suggest you save this for a visit some other time. Access by road is from the A592 Kirkstone Pass road.

(10) It is probable the house was originally built in the sixteenth century but in the mid-nineteenth century the house was developed for a Manchester industrialist by the name of Lingard. What is certain is that the house was again altered and extended by another Manchester industrialist, J. M. Dunlop, who also had the gardens constructed. It is also one of the many

The rooftops of Holehird, with the Coniston fells in the distance.

houses in the Lake District which was rented by Beatrix Potter's father for long summer holidays. It has been used by the Leonard Cheshire organisation for many years and here a team of dedicated carers looks after severely disabled people. Many of the residents have lived there for 40 years and I would hope that this most beautiful of homes has at least partly compensated for their disabilities. I hope you have read about the new Holehird charity in my introduction. The Lakeland Horticultural Society occupies the gardens and here you will find a wonderful collection of plants suited to this area. Members carry out most of the work on a voluntary basis. In particular you should inspect the National Collections of astilbes, hydrangeas and polystichum ferns. Go there to find out more; it's well worth an hour or two of your time. I like to go about four times a year and see the various seasonal delights. Entry is free but visitors should always make a contribution to this garden, which must be one of the most beautifully sited in Britain.

The lawn at the front of Holehird demonstrating the splendid view enjoyed by the residents.

Allen Knott, the site of an Iron Age fort, probably also used by the Romans.

Carrying on up the track you soon come to Far Orrest farm. Here go through the gate on your left and bear right through the small enclosure. Go through another gate and cross the track to another gate, through which you bear right.

> *(11) Up to your left and marked by a power pole is Allen Crag, site of an Iron Age fort which was probably also used by the Romans. If you take a diversion to see it, it takes only five or ten minutes; you may be disappointed since there's precious little to see, but if you have a good imagination and cast your mind back three thousand years you will discern how strategically well placed it was.*

Having turned right, stride on with the wall on your right and then go through the gate on your right, across the track and left, through another gate. The path keeps quite near to the wall on your right before going over a ladder stile. Turn left through the field and then go over another ladder stile and keep following the wall on your left At a corner you will see some stone steps over the wall. Once over these carry on across the pasture to a stile over a fence. A few paces on there is another one before crossing the field and you eventually arrive at the collection of buildings at Near Orrest, some in a state of collapse, where you go through a kissing gate on your right next to a five-barred gate. Bear left through this field and climb over the wall stile onto the road. Here turn right and walk along The Causeway until you almost arrive at The Causeway Farm.

(12) When I first noted the name of this farm, and the road, I was rather puzzled. I'd always connected a causeway with places like St Michael's Mount near Penzance in Mount's Bay, Cornwall, or Lindisfarne off the coast of Northumberland. Both have a 'raised road' leading across the seabed to the island. However, I've since learned that it is so called because it is situated on a raised road, which was a section of the Roman road leading from Kendal to Ambleside. So you may well have been following in the footsteps of Roman legionaries for the last 300 yards. The present main road from Ings to Troutbeck Bridge, passing by Windermere station, is only about 150 years old and was constructed after the coming of the railway, which saw the birth of the town of Windermere in the mid-nineteenth century.

Take the stone steps over the wall next to the gate on your left and bear right to go over a beck. Follow the path through the pasture as it heads towards Orrest Head, which you will see not very far away. There are, seemingly, a multitude of paths but keep as near to the wall as possible and after a while you will find another step-stile over a wall in the corner. You are now at the bottom of the final, sometimes slippery, slope up to Orrest Head and any of the paths you pick will take you up to the top. From this viewpoint (784 ft/238m) you will have a splendid panoramic view of almost the entire length of the lake. There's also a fine collection of seats to enjoy. This view is just one more of the many you will enjoy during the course of this circular walk.

(13) It was to Orrest Head that Alfred Wainwright came on his first, memorable, visit to the Lakes whilst on a day out by train from Blackburn. He was, of course, instantly captivated and spent most of the rest of his life enjoying hundreds of days out on the Lakeland fells and in the dales and capturing the various routes in pen and ink to the delight of millions. The name comes from the old Norse Orrusta *meaning 'a battle' so I assume this is the site of a battle early in the tenth century between the invading Norsemen and the 'English' who were descendents of the Anglo Saxon settlers. The outcrops of stone here are all Silurian Slate, which is the geological name of the underlying*

The view from Orrest Head looking across Windermere towards the Coniston fells.

rock you will encounter during the whole of the walk. The widow and daughter of Arthur Heywood gave Orrest Head to the people of Windermere for public use in 1902.

This part of the walk doesn't finish here, that is three miles further on, but for those who don't want to walk the full 10 miles (16 km) in one day, or if the weather is bad, you can leave the route here and walk into Windermere town. Your day's walk will then have been 5¼ miles (8.4 km). To continue skip the next two description boxes.

To pick up the route at a later stage you will just have to climb back up to the summit of Orrest Head from Windermere town and continue from there, as outlined in the second description box below.

To exit to Windermere

This exit is ¾ mile (1.2 km) long, taking about 20 minutes.

Facing the lake go down the steps ahead of you and down to a kissing gate.

> *(14) When you go through the gate, stop and look at the two tablets of stone, one on either side of the gate. One is a rather flowery but apt Victorian verse. The other tells us that the widow and daughter of Arthur Henry Heywood of Elleray gave Orrest Head to 'the public forever' in 1902. I enjoy the rather flowery phrase: 'in remembrance of the wise and beneficial liberality', which is so redolent of the times, even though I'm not sure what it really means!*

Turn right and, at the end of the fence, turn left to wander down through the trees while still keeping to the left. The path is obvious but you don't want to stray to the right too much. You will find a good track at the bottom of this short stretch through the trees. Follow this past the blacksmith's and in about ten minutes you will be down in Windermere village on the main road from Ambleside.

> *(15) Just before you arrive at the bottom of the track, glance to your right and note the path leading off. This was to be the route of the railway line to Ambleside that William Wordsworth ensured went no further. The Windermere Hotel on your left is one of the oldest buildings in the village of Windermere. It was opened in 1847, the same year that the railway came to the town, which at the time was called Birthwaite. The original station is now incorporated into Booths Supermarket and retains the superb* porte-cochère *station entrance.*

The tourist information office is across the road and so is the station where you can catch a bus or a train.

The kissing gate just below the summit of Orrest Head and the stone, on the left, commemorating the gift of Orrest Head to 'the public for ever'.

To enter from Windermere

This entry is ¾ mile (1.2 km) long, taking about 20 minutes.

The start is next to the Windermere Hotel and opposite the National Westminster Bank on the A591 Kendal to Ambleside road. It is just across the road from the tourist information office and the bus and railway stations. (15)

The signpost points to Orrest Head and you simply follow the well-made track upwards. Having passed the blacksmith's building after 50 yards, turn right and follow the wall on your right and then the path up through the trees. Turn right at the top along the path and pass through the kissing gate to go up the steps to Orrest Head. (14)

Having enjoyed the view, if the weather is clement, face the lake and take the grassy path down on your left.

The old Windermere railway station, now Booth's supermarket, showing the elegant *porte-cochère*.

To continue on to Lindeth Lane stand facing the lake and take the grassy path on your left, which descends gently in a southerly direction to a stone wall. Turn left and follow the path, which may be overgrown by bracken in summer, down to a stile and onto a track. Turn right through the gateway and into the shelter of the trees in Common Wood. At the wall pass through then turn left downhill and after a few strides you pass through a collapsed wall. You may find that the path is not obvious but if you go straight down you will soon pick it up. The path then levels off and you go over a couple of footbridges before rising up slightly and then down again bearing left Go through a gate and into a field and at the other side there is a gate onto a lane. Turn right and walk along the lane to the main Windermere–Kendal road. You have to cross over here and this can be tricky with traffic coming at you quickly over the hill to your right.

(16) This hill is known as Alice Howe and is marked as such on the OS map, but Thomas Jeffrys, the eighteenth-century cartographer, details it as 'Alliss Holme'. Who Alliss or Alice was I don't know, but a howe *is from the Old Norse* haugr *meaning mound or knoll, whereas* holme *is what the islands of Windermere are usually called. So I can only assume Mr Jeffrys was either confused or deaf!*

Once across the road turn right up to the gate on your left. Walk across the field following the track to the gate; then at the end of the next field pass through the high wooden kissing gate on your left and follow the path over the rough ground towards the railway line. Cross over the line taking great care not to step into the path of a train. (Well it's worth a reminder; you could be deep in conversation with a companion) Descend the path opposite, meanwhile glancing over on your left into the very attractive garden at Gill.

(17) The people who named this place were obviously not fans of Wordsworth, but since a 'gill' is a wooded valley we can assume that at one time there were a lot of trees here and the house was built before Wordsworth was around.

At the bottom bear right and then walk along the path at the back of some houses, built in 2000. Cross over the entrance road and take the track left

Pass through the gate ahead and here you have to make a decision, either the higher and longer route up School Knott to your left, which provides another splendid view on a good day, or the lower shorter option. For the lower and shorter option go to the next description box. The longer route goes up the Knott, follow the path up on your left through the young trees.

(18) These trees were planted by the schoolchildren of

The stone below School Knott commemorating the planting of trees on the occasion of the Golden Jubilee of Queen Elizabeth's accession to the Crown.

Windermere to celebrate the Golden Jubilee of Queen Elizabeth II in 2002. They should be looking quite splendid by about the year 2015, or even earlier.

Having climbed up through the plantation, go through the gate and then strike upward and to the right, and when you arrive at a shallow beck step across to take the right-hand path. The 'true' summit is the one on the right. If the visibility is good you will enjoy more superb views from here in all directions (760 ft/232m).

(19) I'm not sure why it is called School Knott but I am sure it was never the location for a school. It is most probably a corruption of the Old English scala, *or* scale, *meaning a shelter. A* knott *is a 'rocky outcrop on a hill', or it could even be from the Old English personal name* Cnotta. *In which case it could be so named because Cnotta had a shelter here. Anyhow whilst you have been thinking about this I hope you've also noticed that the summits surrounding Windermere do indeed provide some memorable vistas and from this one you get a good view of the Howgills and the Pennines to the east, as well as the southern Lakeland fells.*

Carry on over the top and make for School Knott tarn, which you can see below. Pass through the gate and bear right around the edge of the tarn with the slope up on your right. You will soon pick up the path that is in fact the Dales Way, which joins from your left at the next gate. Follow the path down and after emerging past a clump of gorse bushes, where the track is often quite wet, bear left down the grassy slope to the path below.

Windermere town and lake from School Knott, with Orrest Head on the right.

To miss out the climb up to School Knott

This shortens the walk by ½ mile (0.8 km) and by about 20 minutes.

Carry straight on along the path to go past the lovely cottage, called Old Droomer, and follow the lane down and up until it comes to a sharp right-hand bend. Here pass through the gate on your left and follow the path ahead until it comes to the junction with the Dales Way. This is quite soon after you have passed through a gate which often seems to be in the middle of a beck.

The route now carries on along the track.

Follow the track through more gates until it eventually becomes a narrow lane which soon emerges onto the road. You will in fact be almost opposite Windermere golf course. Turn right and go over the stile in the wall to follow the concessionary path for about 130 yards until you emerge out onto the road again near the entrance to Cleabarrow. You now have to walk along the road for ¾ mile (1 km) to the crossroads with Lickbarrow Road on your right and Lindeth Lane on your left. This is a busy road from the Windermere car ferry to Plumgarth roundabout, Kendal and the M6, and cars travel far too fast despite a speed limit of 40 miles per hour. So keep to the right, in single file, keep your eyes on the traffic coming towards you and be prepared to dive to your right at all times!

> *(20) Until the middle of the nineteenth century this road was the packhorse route from Ferry Nab to Kendal, during which time the road would have had up to as many as 50 packhorses slowly plodding along. On your left, over the wall, is Windermere golf course on Undermillbeck Common, which was originally enclosed in 1822 and the land shared by the adjoining landowners. The golf club was founded in 1891 on land leased from the Church of England.*

After walking along this road for about 10–15 minutes you will arrive at a crossroads. If you are doing the next section of the route, turn left into Lindeth Lane, otherwise turn right into Lickbarrow Road.

To exit to Bowness

This exit is 1¼ miles (2 km) long, taking about 45 minutes.

At the crossroads go into Lickbarrow Road and walk up the gentle incline for about 250 yards, then bear left up a track to a high stile over a wall, next to a gate. Follow the track ahead and as you approach Brantfell Farm bear left to follow the indistinct path with the wall on your right. At the top go over the stile on your right, not the one ahead, and go down the slope through the bushes and then bear right again down the pasture. A few steps lead you into another pasture where you bear left. This path is at the right-hand side of the field. It emerges onto a track where you cross over and continue ahead and eventually drop down, with the lake and Bowness in sight, to pass the end of the Dales Way and into Brantfell Road down into the centre of Bowness. Go to the lake shore at Bowness Bay. Here you can catch a bus, or steamer, back to Ambleside.

The end of the Dales Way just above Bowness and looking north up the lake.

Lindeth Lane to Fell Foot

7¾ miles (12.5 km),
approximately 3 hours 15 minutes
Total ascent 1230 ft (375 m)

To enter from Bowness

This entry is 1¼ miles (2 km) long, taking about 45 minutes.

From Bowness Bay walk towards the centre of Bowness and turn right into St Martin's Place, the narrow road opposite St Martin's Church. At the junction with the Lyth Valley road, cross over to go up Brantfell Road to the left of the Spinney restaurant. At the top go over a stile and climb up to pass the start, or end, of the Dales Way. Continue upwards to cross a track and follow the path up through the meadow, with the trees on your left. At the top of this field you will see six steps up on your right. Take the path a short distance up the field and then bear to the left through some trees and over the wall. Follow the indistinct path left close to the wall. Soon you will be on the track leading away from Brantfell Farm and this leads you through fields to Lickbarrow Road.

You may also wish to take the short diversion to the top of Brant Fell 626 ft (191m), where you will get a good view up and down the lake.

Turn right at the road and at the crossroads, go straight across into Lindeth Lane, but do so with great care.

Taking great care crossing over the main road, go in to Lindeth Lane, but even in this much quieter lane still look out for vehicles, the drivers of which will not expect to see you on foot. It is narrow and more winding and uphill, until you come to the entrance to Lindeth Farm on your right.

(21) Most place-names in England which include 'Lind' indicate a connection with lime-trees. It comes from the Anglo-Saxon.

Turn right to go along the track and follow the path between the houses, bearing left. Then you take the track which bears right and passes through the field and leads up to the house. Go through the gate and then bear left past the house to follow the yellow waymarkers and take the left-hand path when you pass through the next gate. This goes through a field and then through another gate before entering into the rough ground of Lindeth Crags. The path is easy to follow but if you keep to the left of the overhead power lines whilst walking through the crags, you are going in the right direction. After three poles the path passes below an outcrop on your right and then bears right, still going down and underneath the power lines, with another outcrop on your left. On top of this outcrop is the third of the power line poles. The path soon brings you to a stile over a wall and on to a lane. Turn right and walk down to the road about 25 yards away.

The 'intake', just off the road near Winster, down which stock would be driven off the pastures of Scout Hill.

The boundary of Westmorland and Lancashire taken from the Lancashire side.

Cross over, go through the gate and follow the 'intake' upwards and, after ascending about 50 yards, turn left and follow the path with the wall on your left and towards the trees. This path can be very muddy after rain. Descending, still with the wall on your left, you pass through a gate and very soon another gate and across a narrow beck, often just a muddy mess. At the signpost turn right up the track.

> *(22) As you emerged from the trees and went through the gate you stepped out of the old county of Westmorland and into the old county of Lancashire. You will in fact be walking in 'Lancashire' until the last mile of the circuit when you cross over the River Brathay as you approach Ambleside. The present administrative county of Cumbria was constituted in 1974.*

Carry on climbing upwards along the track, bearing left at the fork. It levels off for a while and passes footpaths off to your left and right before going downhill through a gate and then upwards on what is now a good surface. Soon there is a reservoir on your right.

> *(23) It always surprises me that there are so many reservoirs surrounding England's biggest lake, but when you think about it*

the people who built them probably found it easier to gather their own water on their own land than have it piped in from public resources. Until the end of the nineteenth century this area and Furness, over the other side of the lake, were highly active in an industrial capacity, there being numerous bobbin mills, bloomeries (iron production) and quarries. This is just one reservoir or dam which would be there to provide water power. The lands here were at one time held by Cartmel Priory but after the Dissolution in 1536 small enclosures were made by local farmers. 250 years later a parliamentary act allowed for the formal enclosure and part of the land on your right became known as Birket Houses Allotment and was given to the owners of the nearby Birket House.

Follow this track, going through a deer-proof gate and eventually over a cattle-grid, out onto Ghyll Head Road. Turn left and walk along the road and after about five minutes you arrive at the junction with Birks Road. Turn left here, passing the entrance to High and Low Moor farms. This is a private road open to the public and although our route passes through the garden of Low Moor you cannot go this way since there is a five-metre gap which is not a public right of way. This is a pity since it is a much easier route. So take the higher right-hand road. This ascends and bends and descends again, passing Low Ludderburn House on your left.

Low Ludderburn, Arthur Ransome's house, 1925–35.

(24) This was the home of Arthur Ransome from 1925 to 1935 and where he wrote the wonderful children's book, Swallows and Amazons, *and others. From the spot where you are now standing it is about 1 mile in a south-westerly direction to Windermere and Blake Holme Island, just off the eastern shore. This is Ransome's 'Wild Cat Island' and about ¾ mile further north up the lake, on the opposite side, is Silver Holme which is 'Cormorant Island' in his most famous children's book. Just to confuse readers he did, of course, also set some of his story at Coniston Water, and it is argued by 'Conistonians' that 'Wild Cat Island' is based on Peel Island; the truth is that the harbour of 'Wild Cat Island' is based on a small cove at the southern end of Peel Island. You will pass close by Silver Holme during Stage 3 up the western shore, during which you will be able to see Blake Holme Island from Stott Park Heights.*

At the bottom of the hill the road turns sharply to the left and on your right look for the signpost pointing to Birks Road. Go through the gate and walk up the track with the boundary on your left. Pass through another gate and as you approach the third gate bear right across the pasture. The track crosses over a beck and then the path bears left to the top left-hand corner of the field, and a field gate with a stile adjacent. In this field bear right up the field towards the wall to pick up a grassy track which soon leads you up to a gate and the farmhouse at Low Moor How.

Go through the gate and past the barn on your right and you will find yellow waymarkers leading you through the garden of the first house; follow the stepping stones to the right over the grass. The path is then left along a short path and through a gate. Go over the stile on your left and then right to pass the front of the next house and go through another gate into a field. Follow the path ahead through the pasture, discernable since the grass is greener, with the slope up to your right. On your right, after a few yards, is a signpost where you walk straight on ahead. Soon you will come to a gate and the path keeps to the right, next to a wall, as you ascend upwards to another gate.

Through this gate the path gets much rougher underfoot as it passes through Moor How Park and in wet weather it can be hard going. You gradually rise up and then drop down to a gate and the stile that leads you into Blake Holme Plantation. Again the path can be quite wet but it is easy to follow as it meanders through the trees. After nearing a high deer fence it gently descends and after about five minutes you arrive at a junction of paths next to Burrow Beck. Turn right and cross over the beck then immediately take the narrow path on your left, through the trees, and follow the ascending path with the beck on your left-hand side. The path keeps quite close to the beck as it gently, then steeply, climbs upwards through the trees. Pass through a clearing, then bear left and soon you will approach a ladder stile over a wall, next to a gate. This leads you out into rough open ground. Follow the path ahead and gently upwards. You will soon come to a fork and here you keep left. Follow the path a minute or two more and then take the left fork again through the bracken heading in the direction of a tall, single larch tree. The path soon comes to a fallen wall and you step through and over this to carry straight on ahead. It may be rather tough going here since it is quite overgrown in summer, and quite boggy too. At the next junction there is a collection of loose slate on the slope on your right and a tree on your left. Take the path

Looking north along Windermere from Gummer's How towards the snow-capped central fells.

The view west across Windermere towards Finsthwaite Heights and the village of Finsthwaite nestling below.

sharply to the right and upward. After a few yards take the left-hand path steeply upwards towards the summit of Gummer's How. In good visibility you will soon see the 'trig point' on the top, but if it's misty just keep going up. A lot of paths have developed and they all lead you where you want to go. You have now arrived at the highest point on *Windermere: Walking around the Lake* (1025 ft/313m).

(25) Hopefully you will appreciate another splendid view of the Lakeland fells to the north and west. You may also enjoy more good views of the eastern Fflls: the Howgills, the Pennines, Ingleborough and, towards the south-east, the relatively low range of the Bowland Fells. Also you should see almost the whole length of the lake from a different perspective, and much of the route that you have already walked. You may find it hard to believe that only 200 years ago most of the trees you see around the lake would not have been there, most of the surrounding land being rough grassland grazed bare by sheep. The name Gummer's How is derived from the Old English and means 'a hill owned by a man called Godmund'. To the south you may also be able to see the expanse of Morecambe Bay and the Kent estuary at Arnside. The River Kent passes through

Kendal. To the south-west you may be able to see the tower on Hoad hill, a lighthouse-like structure overlooking Ulverston. It was constructed to commemorate Sir John Barrow, who was born in Ulverston in 1764. It is in the style of a former Eddystone lighthouse and celebrates his career as the Second Secretary to the Admiralty. He is best remembered for his support of the exploration of the Arctic and the Northwest Passage.

Enjoy the view and then carefully descend by taking the path that takes you steeply down the craggy outcrop in a southerly direction. It may not be too obvious but it will become clear when you search for it. I find that it's quite often a bit tricky leaving the summit of a fell and taking the right path. If you have a compass it's due south but otherwise just descend as best you can and the track you're looking for is well maintained. There's a good chance someone will be coming up it anyhow. After about ten minutes you will pass through a wall and find yourself on a road. Turn right and follow it steeply downhill for a kilometre until it meets the Newby Bridge–Windermere road. Turn right on the main road and soon, on your left, you will arrive at the National Trust's Fell Foot Park.

If you have done these sections in one straight walk you will have walked 16¼ miles.

Lakeside seen from across Windermere at Fell Foot.

Take the NT ferry across to Lakeside if you are carrying on the circular walk.

Here you can catch a bus back to Windermere and Ambleside (hopefully you will have checked the timetable for the bus and the steamer and launch timetable before you set off). On the other hand you can walk down to the shop, café and landing stage. Take the NT ferry across to Lakeside and board the steamer or launch to go back up the lake to Bowness or Ambleside. If you decide on the bus, stand in a visible place at the side of the road and make sure you hold your hand out to stop the bus. Stand where the bus driver has a good view of you. A good place is opposite the red post box where the road levels off and there is a quite good verge.

Lakeside, looking north along Windermere with Gummer's How on the right.

Lakeside to the Ferry House

6¾ miles (10.2 km),
approximately 3 hours 45 minutes
Total ascent 1156 ft (352m)

I'm assuming that you will start this sector from Lakeside and will have arrived on the steamer, but I'm well aware that you may have arrived by car and parked at Lakeside. You could even have parked at Fell Foot and come across on the little ferry. This is the cheapest option if there are only two of you and you are NT members. You will, of course, have to make your way back here if you have left a car.

(26) Lakeside is a product of the Victorian tourist boom, created by the linking of the railway with the lake steamers. Tourists would travel by coach and horse, later by tram, from Blackpool to Fleetwood and then sail across Morecambe Bay to Barrow from where they would take a train to Lakeside. From Lakeside they would sail up to Waterhead and back and then return to Blackpool. Quite a long day out and no doubt an exciting one for the Lancashire mill workers who formed the bulk of the visitors. Here there is a splendid aquarium which is well worth a visit some time, probably not today though, and the steam train journey to Haverthwaite and back is quite an experience too. At Lakeside there is good provision for refreshments and a comfort break before you start your walk. There isn't anywhere else until the end of the day.

So to start the walk leave the car park and go past the entrance to the Lakeside Hotel on to the Newby Bridge–Hawkshead road. Turn right and walk along the road, taking care to watch out for traffic. After about 300 yards, or about 5 minutes, there is a footpath on the left-hand side of the road going up through trees and leading to Finsthwaite.

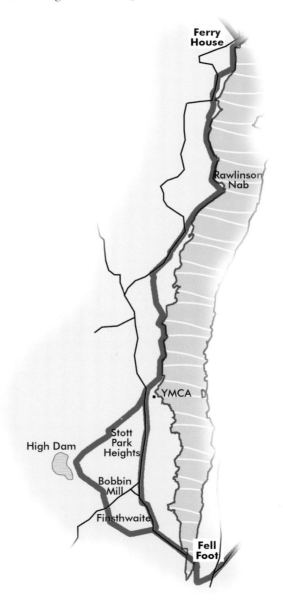

**Ferry
House**

Rawlinson
Nab

YMCA

Stott
Park
Heights

High Dam

Bobbin
Mill

Finsthwaite

**Fell
Foot**

Here you have to make a decision: higher and longer, with the ascent up to High Dam and Stott Park Heights; or lower and shorter on the road.

The high level route involves an ascent of about 350 ft/105m, followed by a short descent and then another climb of 195 ft/60m, followed by a descent back to the road you are now on but about a mile to the north. If you opt for the lower route and follow the road you will miss out on the views across the lake from Stott Heights to Gummer's How and Blake Island, not to mention missing the attractive environs of High Dam. It is, however, one mile shorter and you will also save about 50 minutes. For directions, go to the next description box in two pages.

So if you have decided on the longer route, cross over taking care, and climb up the track through Great Knott Wood. Soon you will be at the top and the path emerges into a field, where you head across in the direction of the church. After walking through two fields you will go through a gate and find yourself on another track, which passes the church.

Finsthwaite churchyard. The memorial is to Clemintina Johannes Sobieski Douglas, the 'Finsthwaite Princess'

(27) The present church of St Peter, built in 1874, replaced a much older chapel. There is an interesting grave in the church-yard. It is a grave with a cross next to a 'table grave' on the opposite side of the church to the porch. This is the resting place of Clementina Johannes

The still waters of High Dam reservoir on a cold, crisp winter's day.

Sobiesky Douglass who died on 16 May 1771 and who, it is suggested, was an illegitimate daughter of Prince Charles Edward Stuart, popularly known as Bonnie Prince Charlie. Why she lived and died here is a matter of conjecture. The facts do seem to have a semblance of truth since Prince Charles' mother was named Maria Clementina and was the granddaughter of King John Sobieski of Poland. Douglas was the family name of Charles. It is an intriguing mystery and if you want to follow it up there is a booklet published by the Cumberland and Westmorland Antiquarian and Archaeological Society entitled The Finsthwaite Princess: the making of a myth *written by Janet D. Martin. Just as a matter of interest, in another St Peter's, the Basilica of St Peter in Rome, there is an enormous monument above the tomb of Maria Clementina Sobieski, the wife of James Stuart, the Old Pretender. It reaches about 25-feet high and is set between two marble columns, quite near the entrance. Could there be a greater contrast between the memorials to two such similarly named women?*

Leaving the church go straight up the lane opposite into the centre of the village, next to the house with the interesting balcony.

(28) This small hamlet is an ancient place named after a man called Finn, a Norseman who had a farmstead in the clearing here, a thwaite being the Norse for 'clearing'. You will notice that the village is still surrounded by trees and is probably not a lot different in its setting, apart from the houses here, than it was a thousand years ago.

At the junction turn right and after a few yards take the indicated path on your left, up past a few cottages and over a stile into a field. You should see waymarkers here and you follow these, but essentially you are going straight on to ascend through the first field, and the next heading for the trees. Cross over a beck and turn left to wend your way gradually upward, keeping the beck on your left. In a few minutes, after a stiff ascent, you will come to a small dam. The beck you've walked alongside, or at least near to, comes down from this. Carry on upwards to a bigger dam, High Dam (567 ft/173m), and the delightful reservoir which, I believe, is one of the Lake District's hidden gems, even though it is man made.

(29) You can't help but notice that the dam holds a considerable amount of water and it would certainly have been sufficient to power Stott Park Bobbin Mill, situated lower down near the lake. See also Note 31 on page 49.

It's possible to walk around the reservoir in a clockwise direction. Just walk across the dam and follow the footpath, with the water down on your right. It takes about 20 minutes and it's well worth the time

Approaching Stott Park Heights from High Dam reservoir.

if you think you can spare it. At the end of the circuit you pass through a gateway and soon bear left on the track to pass though a kissing gate and you are back on route.

If you decide not go around the reservoir, bear right over the footbridge and walk along the path with the dam down on your left Carry on along this path but bear right at the fork and the path passes through a kissing gate and gradually downwards over rough ground, though the path is good underfoot. Ahead you will see a massive outcrop and this is Stott Park Heights, your next objective. At the bottom cross over the beck, bear left and follow the path as it wends its way clockwise upwards through holly trees, Scots pines and others, with the heather covered, craggy outcrop of Stott Park Heights up on your right. As it levels out somewhat look for a track leading up through the bracken; don't worry there are a number of these and they all lead you to the top. At the top the heather is everywhere and a narrow path wends its way eastwards towards the lake over about three linear outcrops of rock running north to south. You may, like me, be a little amused by the name 'Heights' because it is only 636 ft/193m above sea level. I'm sure you will agree, however, that it is a good viewpoint to admire the surrounding fells and the lake.

The view east from Stott Park Heights across the lake to Gummer's How. Blake Holme island is just visible at the right hand edge of the photograph.

(30) You will find a bench here which is a good place to have a coffee or lunch break, or just a few minutes' rest, during which period you may see and, undoubtedly hear, one or two supersonic jets scream past below you. Look across Windermere and see 'Wild Cat Island', Blake Holme Island, just to your left against the opposite shore and, up above, Gummer's How is just to your right by about 10 degrees.

Leaving Stott Park Heights go to the left down the steep slope and find the narrow path on which you ascended earlier. This goes down to your right, at first steeply. You will arrive at a dilapidated wall and, perhaps, an orienteering post if it's still there. Turn left and down with the wall on your right. After 50 yards go through a break in the wall and down steeply, following the rather rugged and steeply descending path which is not easy to pick out. It's been lined with fallen branches and there are occasional steps and it zigzags two or three times before approaching a beck, which will be on your left as you go down the slope. Stride over and through another dilapidated wall. The descent becomes more gradual and in a few minutes you will pass through a gate where you continue ahead and soon find you have descended back down to the road you left earlier.

Low level route

This shortens the walk by ¾ mile (1.2 km) and about 50 minutes. The ascent will also be 541 ft (164 m) less.

So, having decided to stay lower down, continue along the road, still taking care, and after about 600 yards you will come to Stott Park Bobbin Mill.

(31) This is well worth a couple hours of your time, perhaps on another occasion. It was just one of many mills in this area which produced bobbins for the cotton mills further south in Lancashire. Trees growing in this area were especially coppiced to produce the right sort of timber for these bobbins, as well as used for producing charcoal. The bark was also often used in the process of tanning. The mill operated

Stott Park bobbin mill, 1835–1971. Now an English Heritage working museum.

from 1835 until 1971. In 1983 English Heritage purchased the remains and it has become a working museum, where you can see how a typical mill of this type operated. The original steam engine is still in situ *and can be seen working, although the machinery is now powered by electricity.*

Carry on a further 450 yards and, just past the house at High Stott Park, you will find a permissive path on your right. Follow this and later change over to the other side until you come to the YMCA centre. This is where the longer route meets up.

Cross over the road, turn left and pass the entrance to the YMCA complex. Soon you will find a footpath on your right and in a minute or two for the first time on *Windermere: Walking Around the Lake* you will be actually walking alongside the shore of the lake. Having walked along the lake shore for about two minutes you will soon pass a promontory called Long Tongue and then the small islet of Silver Holme ('Cormorant Island'), after which the path goes inland for a few yards to go round Newlands Cottage. The path then follows a good track and soon your lake side stroll is over for about another mile. At a boathouse the track goes left and steadily upwards through the trees of Boathouse Wood and High Cat Crag – not named by Arthur Ransome! Soon you emerge onto the Newby Bridge–Hawkshead road again (340 ft/103m). Turn right and walk steeply downhill. Having descended 145 ft/45m the road gradually climbs uphill again until, at a corner, you will find a path on your right next to Holme Well house. So go over the stile and soon you are on the lake shore again and in a few minutes you will come to another promontory, Rawlinson Nab, which is much bigger than Long Tongue. You may wish to have a rest here and enjoy the views across and up and down the lake.

> *(32) The Rawlinsons were a local family who owned a lot of land and many properties hereabouts, the nearby Graythwaite Hall and Old Graythwaite Hall being just two of them. The Nab was also one of Thomas West's recommended 'Viewing Stations' in his book* Guide to the Lakes *published in 1778.*

Leaving the Nab, the path keeps very close to the shore and sometimes you may even think you're walking in the lake. It can be wet under foot here when the lake is full after heavy and prolonged rainfall. Then you will find another islet just offshore, Ling Holme, before you pass over Cunsey Beck and arrive at a stile and then a boathouse and quay on your right. Continue on along the path that is still very near to the water until you leave the water's edge again and approach a small bungalow, The Bield, and a stile where once more you must climb over on to the road. Bear right and this time it's quite a short stretch of about 700 yards before you take the track going down on your right. This is a private road but don't be put off since what it doesn't tell you is that that it is a permissive path for people on foot – but not on bikes. This brings you down near the shoreline again and then out onto the Car Ferry–Hawkshead road at Ash Landing. Taking care, cross over and go into the car park and follow the waymarkers to the ferry. When you come back out onto

Looking south down the lake from Rawlinson Nab.

the road, if you are doing the circular route turn left ignoring the road to the ferry, and go to the next description box. If you are ending your walk, take the road to the ferry to go into Bowness.

The car ferry takes 10 minutes (though you may have to wait half an hour for it) and it is ¾ mile (1.2 km) from Ferry Nab to Bowness, 45 minutes, including ferry.

Take the car ferry, or alternatively a launch which takes you direct to Bowness Bay in 15 minutes. Look for the launch landing stage on the water's edge, where there should be a timetable displayed, but the launch doesn't run in winter and runs about once every hour in season. If you travel back on the car ferry this runs all year round, about once every 15–20 minutes during the day. Check on the starting and stopping times of the car ferry, though it does run until mid-evening all year round. At the other side walk along the road for about 200 yards, then turn left, past the kiosk, and continue straight on to follow the path into Bowness. This soon crosses Glebe Road and continues with the pitch-and-putt course on your left and the cemetery on your right, emerging through a coach park to Bowness Bay. This takes 15–20 minutes and is about ¾ mile (1.2 km). If you have managed to take the launch direct to Bowness the journey time is about 10 minutes.

To enter from Bowness

This exit is ¾ mile (1.2 km) to Ferry Nab, taking about 45 minutes including the car ferry. The direct launch to the Ferry House runs in summer about once every hour and takes about 15 minutes.

From Bowness Bay find the Tourist Information Centre, which is on your right with your back towards the lake and on the corner of Glebe Road. Go into the coach park next to the TIC and at the far end find a lane which passes between the pitch-and-putt golf course and the cemetery. Cross the road and through the opposite gate and at the far end carry straight on and past a kiosk and at the road turn right to Ferry Nab.

The Ferry House to Ambleside

7 miles (11.20 km),
approximately 3 hours 30 minutes
Total ascent 660 ft (201m)

The starting point for this stage is at the junction where the road comes from the car ferry. On the other hand you may wish to leave your car at Ash Landing NT car park, though getting back to it will involve taking a launch or steamer from Ambleside to Bowness and then walking back and crossing on the car ferry. This lane can be rather busy and it is also narrow, so watch out for cars, the drivers of which should in fact be watching out for you but don't bank on it.

Once again a decision has to be made: it is a question of a higher and longer, or a lower and shorter route.

The high level route is about ¾ mile (1.2 km) further and involves a total ascent of 740 ft/225m. It will also take about an hour longer than the lower route directly alongside the lake. This high level route

Looking across Mitchell Wyke to the Ferry House.

provides occasional glimpses of the lake, Bowness and the eastern route above Bowness. For details of this higher level route go to the next description box.

Walk down the lane from the ferry. You are now passing Mitchell Wyke, a sheltered corner of the lake popular with boat owners, and you will notice the wide variety of craft anchored here.

(33) It is also, incidentally, the place where I first remember coming to Windermere when I was about 15 years old. I stayed overnight on a boat by the name of Marshall Soult, *just one of many motor cruisers ('The Little Ships', as they became known) which answered the call to rescue British troops from the shores of France at Dunkirk in 1940. I must have enjoyed that first visit since I keep coming back to Windermere and the Lakes. Every time I drop down over Alice Howe into Windermere I still get the same feeling of excitement that I had when I made my first visit all those years ago. (This information is, of course, of absolutely no interest to you!)*

You will be very near to the lake for the next 2½ miles (4 km). After the track enters the trees further on, and where the good surface ends, you will not be directly next to the water all the time. So if you wish to stop and rest this next mile is quite a good place to do so. It is, however, also popular with a variety of water birds – Canada geese in particular, and they can make rather a foul mess on the greensward so be careful where you rest your posterior.

(34) Directly opposite is Windermere's largest island, Belle Isle, which is about 1000 yards (1 kilometre) in length. There are also two adjacent small islands just off the shore, known as the Lilies of the Valley. Belle Isle was originally called Langholme – meaning 'long island' – but was purchased by a John English who built the round house in 1774, which you may glimpse hiding amongst the trees. Isabel Curwen bought it prior to her marriage to John Christian, who subsequently took the name Curwen. Up on your left is Heald Wood on the slopes of Claife Heights. Claife *comes from the Old Norse and means 'steep hill-side up which there is a path'. Obvious, isn't it! The bigger island to the north is Thompson's Holme.*

Looking up the lake with Belle Isle on the right, Lilies of the Valley and Thompson Holme. In the distance the distinctive peak of Ill Bell can be seen overlooking upper Troutbeck.

Carrying on along the track, you soon come to a cattle-grid and gate; go into the shade of the tree canopy and you will find the surface of the path underfoot rather more rugged. It is still a road open to vehicles and of course is popular with cyclists. However, it's a pleasant walk and after passing a small caravan site you will find the track climbing up and away from the lake side and then gently dropping down again. After about a mile (20 minutes) you will arrive at Belle Grange.

High level route

This lengthens the walk by ¾ mile (1.2 km) and about 50 minutes. The ascent will also be 593 ft (181m) more.

Instead of following the lake side road north, find the signpost to take the footpath up the rather steep slope following the white route as indicated. However, to be sure you follow the correct route I will also describe it here. Climb up the track until you come to an old ruin.

(35) This is a viewing station constructed in the late eighteenth century by one of the Curwen's of Belle Isle for the

51

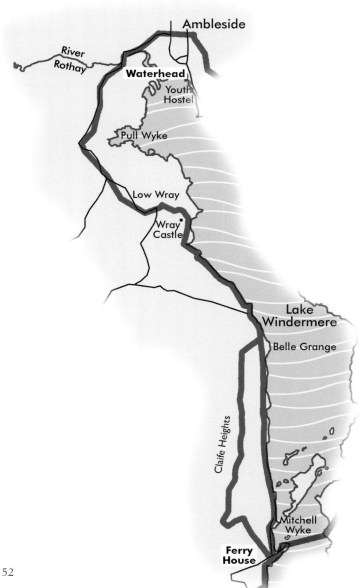

The ruins of the eighteenth-century viewing station just above the lake and the Ferry House.

use of those of a 'romantic persuasion', who toured the Lake District taking in the 'breathtaking and sometimes frightening views'. There is an explanation on a couple of boards attached to the walls. Various writers of tour guides had equally varying opinions. Thomas West, author of A Guide to the Lakes, *held it in high regard, whilst the Frenchman, Louis Simond, author of* A journal of a tour and residence in Great Britain *during 1810 and 1811, wrote: '... Affords no favourable specimen of proprietor's taste ...' Simond was married to an English-woman, the niece of John Wilkes, the great eighteenth-century journalist and politician.*

From here climb up the path which, as you ascend, provides good views of Belle Isle and across the lake to Bowness. The path passes through a rocky outcrop and is quite steep in parts, then levels out somewhat as it traverses the slope, often scrambling over another set of rocky outcrops and more or less following the contour line. Eventually you walk through trees and pass through a kissing gate onto a bridleway. Here, turn left and follow the track for about 250 yards. Turn right at the finger post, painted white at the top with a number 3 on it, and on which should be affixed a map outlining the white route. Follow this path as it gently undulates along the

Bowness, Belle Isle and School Knott viewed from the lookout on Low Pate Crag.

crest of Claife Heights, though there is one short steep descent, followed by a similar ascent. At 'Junction 4' don't turn left but carry straight on with an old wall on your right and a gap in the wall leads to Low Pate Crag.

You may wish to stop a while and go to the lookout where you will have a splendid view up and down the lake. Directly below you can see to Belle Isle and Bowness and across to School Knott, and if you move about a bit you will also spot Orrest Head and other features of the eastern route.

Return to the path, turn right and follow the undulating path, soon passing right through the wall, when the path offers more good views of the lake and across to the eastern route and to the distant Howgill Fells. This path takes you along the part of Claife Heights known as The Heald for about a mile before crossing a ford and the well-paved bridleway, which was the packhorse route between Hawkshead and the lake. Here turn right, downhill, to Belle Grange where you turn left and pick up the lower, lake side, route.

(36) At one time a ferry plied across the lake from Millerground on the opposite shore to connect to the packhorse trail which climbs up Claife Heights en route *to Hawkshead.*

However, we are doing a 'round the lake walk' so carry on and the path comes close to the shoreline again and leaves the cover of the trees. About 300 yards further on you pass through a gate and arrive at Red Nab car park. On your right you will find a bridleway following the shore again. So, ignoring the road which climbs up to the left, take the bridleway as it wends its way in and out of trees during this particularly pleasant sector of the walk and with the lake close by on your right-hand side. Eventually you will pass through a gate and arrive at High Wray Bay. After a few strides go through another gate. The path now goes upwards and away from the lake. So at the second gate on your right leave the track, pass through the gate and follow the path along the pasture, with the shoreline down on your right. After a while it bears left away from the water to go up the slope, and then bears right. Soon you come to a stile and a gate into

Looking west across the lake to Belle Grange from Millerground. This is not a view you will see on the walk.

Wray Castle, the 'Hollywoodesque' castle erected during the 1840s for a Liverpool doctor.

a plantation. Don't go over this but turn left uphill towards Wray Castle and pass through a gate.

(37) When you arrive at the castle, now owned by the National Trust, you will realise that it is not a real castle but a 'Hollywoodesque' construction, no doubt someone's idea of what a castle should look like. In reality it is an early Victorian building, constructed between 1840–47, for a Liverpool doctor for the grand sum of £60,000. In 1892 a certain Rupert Potter rented the castle for his family's summer holiday. So this is another summer home of Beatrix Potter. The castle is currently leased and used as a training college. One of the founders of the National Trust, Canon Rawnsley, had been Vicar of Wray but by that time he was the Vicar of Crossthwaite, near Keswick. The name Wray *comes from the Old Norse for 'corner', though I'm not sure how Wray can be described as being in a corner.*

Having passed through the gate, walk up to the summerhouse and pass the castle to follow the 'Exit' signs to the entrance drive. Just past the Dower House B & B take the track on your right and follow this down to Low Wray Farm

> *(38) The camping site here is the only one open to the public which is situated almost on the lake side and with access to the shore for those who wish to take advantage of this splendid National Trust facility. Going back to my youth, it is a site where I camped with my friends during quite a few Whitsuntide holidays; replaced now by the Spring Bank Holiday. It's also the place where I brought my wife for her first camping experience. It rained and blew but despite that we have enjoyed many more nights under canvas since we slept in that ancient bell-tent, with central pole, which kept the rain off us most efficiently and*

Holy Trinity church at Brathay where the popular wedding hymn *O Perfect Love* was first sung.

stayed upright whilst others were having a rather unpleasant time.

Turn left to stride up the track and onto the road. Almost opposite the farm entrance there is a gate. This leads you to a permissive path, which follows the wall on your right and with the road over on the other side. After about 600 yards you approach some trees and the path leads you through another gate on to the road again. Turn left and walk up to the junction where the road to the left goes to Hawkshead. Carry straight on and near to the next junction look for the entrance to another permissive path on your right through the wall. It's about 20 yards past the gatehouse and entrance to Huyton Hill. This path keeps you off the road until you come to Pull Wyke and here you walk along the pavement until you once again take a permissive path, found at the entrance to a track, for another 100 yards. Cross over the road and take the continuation of the path, turning right with the road over the wall on your right. A stile eventually leads you out of the cover of the trees and you will find yourself on a path between a fence and the wall.

(39) As you emerge from the trees you will see the slopes of Loughrigg Fell ahead of you, and nestling below and just a little to your left is a church. It's called Holy Trinity and is built in the Italianate style. It is otherwise unremarkable but for the fact that due to the difficulties of the site it is not properly orientated, since it doesn't point east as most churches built before the twentieth century did. Giles Redmayne of Brathay Hall founded the church in 1836 and it was for the wedding of his grandson, Dr Hugh Redmayne, in 1883 that the words of the popular wedding hymn O Perfect Love *were written by the bride's sister, Dorothy Blomfield.*

The path ends at Brathay, near to the eponymous river, and once again you take to the road. So bear right, keeping on the left with the river down below, and approach the bridge. This is a very dangerous spot for walkers so negotiate this as safely as you can and climb up to Clappersgate and the Ambleside–Coniston road (A593). As you cross the bridge you pass out of old Lancashire and into old Westmorland. Turn right and walk along the roadside path towards

Ambleside. As you approach Rothay Bridge you will be on another permissive path and you cross the river Rothay on the footbridge. This soon emerges onto a road, bear right and walk up to the junction with the rugby club on your right. Turn right and walk alongside the road back to Waterhead, or turn left to walk into Ambleside. Or, if you want to go back to Fisherbeck car park, cross over the road and go along the path straight ahead which emerges onto Lake Road, the Ambleside–Windermere road, next to the Log House restaurant and opposite is the Fisherbeck car park.

You have now completed *Windermere: Walking around the Lake* and I trust you found it both enjoyable and worthwhile. Perhaps you will think about doing it 'widdershins', or anti-clockwise, sometime?

The Anti-Clockwise Route

For a variety of reasons you may decide that you would rather walk around Lake Windermere in an anti-clockwise direction. Therefore I have written the instructions so that you can do that. In many ways it's a totally different walk, even though you are visiting all the same places. The main difference is that you are, of course, generally facing and looking in a different direction. You will be heading south instead of north on the western side of the lake and looking north instead of south on the eastern side.

I have walked all the stages numerous times and it never ceases to amaze me how different it can during the various seasons of the year. You may be surprised to learn that my favourite season is winter, when the leaves are off the deciduous trees, thereby providing views not seen in summer. My next favourite time is spring, or could it be autumn, followed by summer. I do like summer of course since there is always something special about finding a sunny spot for a picnic, or just lazing in the sun. It being the Lake District, this pleasure isn't just as predictable as further south in England but the weather around Windermere is probably the best in the whole of the Lake District.

The instructions do not include the 'points of interest', which are included in the text for the clockwise route. Should you want to refer to these I have inserted the paragraph numbers in the appropriate place. So to find out more about your walk you will need to turn to the relevant page where you will find this information. You may find some of this slightly confusing but all you need to do is to remember that it was written for people going in the opposite direction. So all you have to do is to turn round and face the direction you have come from and all will be clear – I hope!

Waterhead to Ferry House

7 miles (11.2 km),
approximately 3 hours 30 minutes
Total ascent 631 ft (192m)

Starting from Waterhead with your back to the lake follow the road to the left past the Waters Edge Hotel, and later Borrans Park, with the Roman camp at its far side. At Ambleside Rugby Club bear left and take the footpath on your left as the road bends to the right. Cross over the bridge and turn left

To enter from Ambleside

The additional distance is negligible.

If you are starting at the Fisherbeck car park, on Lake Road in Ambleside, cross over the road and take the footpath to the left of the Log House restaurant. Follow this to the road and cross over, with the rugby pitch just opposite. Take the road towards Hawkshead, Coniston and Langdale and soon you will see a footpath on your left which takes you across a footbridge over the River Rothay, then turn left when you are across.

Walk along the roadside to Clappersgate and turn left, down the road, and over the bridge, towards Hawkshead. This is a rather dangerous bridge so take care. As soon as possible cross over to the right side of the road, with the River Brathay down on your right-hand side. The road bends to the left, to Hawkshead, and you will see the entry to a permissive path on the right-hand corner of the road; another lane leads to Skelwith Fold and the church. (39)

Go through the gate and onto the path, with the wall on your left. Follow this for about 500 yards and soon you will be in the cover of trees. After a while the path crosses to the other side of the road and after 100 yards it emerges onto the roadside, where you keep to the narrow footpath. After about 150 yards look for a narrow gap in the wall on your left and go down steps to the path, with the wall up on your right. This is about 500 yards in length and soon you will emerge out onto the road again, so turn left and keep left at the junction to follow the road towards Wray. At the next junction keep left again and after about another 500 yards you will find a permissive path on the right-hand side. You will be pleased to know this is the end of the boring part of the walk.

Follow this permissive path with the wall on your left-hand side as far as you can go. Don't take the exit through the first gate on your left, where the footpath junction indicates a path off to the right to Blelham Tarn and Outgate. Continue for another 100 yards or so and the path emerges onto the road at Low Wray. Cross over to walk down the lane to Low Wray farm and NT campsite. (38)

As you approach the farm take the path up on your right and follow this track until it leads you to the entrance drive to Wray Castle. Turn left and walk past the Dower House B & B to Wray Castle. (37)

The path takes you round the front of the castle, past a conservatory, and then ahead you will see a gate. Go through and head down the slope and at the bottom turn right. The path soon bends left and goes downwards, nearer to the shoreline. Having followed the shoreline

Approaching Wray Castle from the lake.

Looking across the lake towards Orrest Head from Red Nab.

you soon approach High Wray Bay and a kissing gate, which leads you onto a lane. Turn left and pass through another gate, soon followed by another one, and walk alongside the lake on the well-made track. Beware of cyclists! Soon you arrive at Red Nab car park; carry on and pass through the gate ahead and follow the track which soon brings you to Belle Grange. This is where the old ferry used to cross from Millerground on the eastern shore of Windermere, and the packhorse track to Hawkshead goes up to your right. (36)

Alternative: you have an option here to deviate from the route and take a higher and longer route.

You have to decide if you wish to keep to the lower lake side path, or climb up to take the higher route which leads you along the length of Claife Heights to the car ferry. For the highter route, go to the next description box.

If not taking up the higher route option continue straight on with the lake down on your left. The path is quite uneven for about a mile but you may encounter a car and, almost certainly, cyclists. Passing through a gate/cattle-grid the surface improves and you will be closer to the lake. (34)

This is good place to take a rest but be careful where you sit. This is a favourite place for Canada geese and other waterfowl and they don't care where they deposit their mess. Follow the lane until it passes quite close to the water at Mitchell Wyke. (33)

After a few more paces you are at a junction and left takes you to the car ferry or launch back to Bowness.

High level route

This lengthens the walk by ¾ mile (1 km) and about an hour. The ascent will also be 654 ft (199m) more.

Turn right and climb up the well-made bridleway towards Hawkshead and after a few bends you will come to a signpost. Take the left-hand path which indicates the way to Far Sawrey and the car ferry. This route provides intermittent glimpses of the lake down below where you find the viewpoints. I think it's well worth while taking the opportunity of enjoying the views. You will also be able to look across to the eastern shore and the places you will visit on the eastern route, such as School Knott and Orrest Head. Don't be tempted to take any right-hand turns or left-hand turns, just keep straight on. If you do take the right-hand turns, often indicated by white-tipped posts, make sure you follow the white route. If you take the left-hand paths you will end up on the lower route; so if

One of the white-topped signposts on the high level route across Claife Heights.

Looking up the packhorse route from Belle Grange and over Claife Heights to Hawkshead.

you do go wrong you will not get lost, I hope! The path is undulating and there is at least one descent of about 100 ft (30 m) followed by a similar ascent. Eventually the path emerges from the trees and you will find yourself on a track between stone walls, with fields over on each side. After about five minutes you come to a junction of paths and here you turn sharp left. After about 300 yards keep your eyes open for a kissing gate on your right as the track starts to head downhill. Go through and follow this path, which first passes through trees and then contours round, with the slope down on your left providing good views across the lake and to Belle Isle near to the eastern shore. Having negotiated a rather craggy stretch of path it eventually starts to drop steeply down, with a few bends and in places quite good steps, and you come to the ruin of a viewing station. (35)

Follow the path, which is now well made and wide having been constructed to take carriages, down to the road and the Ferry House.

Both routes end here.

If you are not walking the entire western shore in one stage follow the signpost to the car ferry, or launch, to Bowness Bay.

To exit to Bowness

This exit is ¾ mile (1.2 km) long, taking about 45 minutes, including the ferry. The car ferry takes 10 minutes (though you may have to wait half an hour for it).

Take the car ferry, or alternatively a launch, which takes you direct to Bowness Bay in 15 minutes. Look for the launch landing stage on the water's edge, where there should be a timetable displayed, but the launch doesn't run in winter and runs about once every hour in season. If you travel back on the car ferry this runs all year round, about once every 15–20 minutes during the day. Check on starting and stopping times of the car ferry, though it does run until mid-evening throughout the year. At the other side walk along the road for about 200 yards, then turn left past the kiosk, and continue straight on to follow the path into Bowness. This soon crosses Glebe Road and continues with the pitch-and-putt course on your left and the cemetery on your right, emerging through a coach park to Bowness Bay. This takes 15–20 minutes and is about ¾ mile (1.2 km). If you have managed to take the launch direct to Bowness the journey time is about 10 minutes.

The Ferry House to Lakeside

6.75 miles (10.2 km),
approximately 3 hours 45 minutes
Total ascent 1159 ft (353m)

To enter from Bowness

This entry is ¾ mile (1.2 km) to Ferry Nab, taking about
45 minutes including the car ferry. The direct launch to the
Ferry House runs in summer about once every hour and
takes about 15 minutes.

From Bowness Bay find the tourist information centre, which is on
your right with your back towards the lake and on the corner of
Glebe Road. Go into the coach park next to the TIC and at the far
end find a lane which passes between the pitch-and-putt golf
course and the cemetery. Cross the road and through the opposite
gate, and at the far end carry straight on and past a kiosk. At the
road turn right to Ferry Nab.

At the other side of the lake follow the road from the ferry to the
junction. Walk south along the road from the junction with the road
to and from the car ferry, and with the lake on your left-hand side.
Here the left-hand side of the road is better, since the vehicles leaving
the ferry all come at once. If you have just arrived on the ferry you
will know that the vehicles have all gone and there won't be any
more for at least another 15 minutes. If you are carrying straight on
from Stage 1 then you will have to keep an eye open for traffic
coming off the ferry.

Looking north up the lake from Rawlinson Nab.

In a minute or two the road leaves the lake side and goes uphill towards Hawkshead and the Sawreys, but you take the track on your left, a private road through trees which is open for those on foot. The lake will be on your left and soon the path turns away from the lake and upwards to emerge onto a lane. Turn left, walk along the lane for about 400 yards and at a right-hand bend take the stile on your left. Bear left and down towards the lake where you bear right and follow the footpath alongside the shoreline. It can sometimes be rather wet underfoot here after a lot of rain and when the lake becomes full. In fact wet underfoot could well be an understatement; you could almost be walking in the lake! Soon you come to a boathouse and you go over the wall by using the step-stile. Next you stride over Cunsey Beck and offshore is Ling Holme. Carrying on, you next walk round Rawlinson Nab, which is another pleasing place to stop and enjoy a rest. (32)

Leaving Rawlinson Nab the path follows the lake shore for another 500 yards before you take to the road again. So turn left, after having gone over the elaborate stile, and follow the road downhill for about ¾ mile (1.2km) before it climbs steeply up again. As you near the top look carefully for a footpath on your left which goes up a step or two to go through the wall and into trees. The path now descends High Cat Crag through the trees of Boat House Wood to ... a boathouse! Turn right and follow the track, which is now beside the lake again. It goes round the back of a house on the water's edge to get back to the shore. First you pass Silver Holme just off the shore. (24) This note may be a bit confusing since it is written to read on the clockwise route whilst on the eastern path, but I think you'd rather have this information now than later in the walk.

Next pass a small promontory aptly called Long Tongue. In another 600 yards the path leaves the shoreline again; the last time you walk alongside the shoreline of Windermere for the rest of the circuit. Look across the lake and south to see Blake Holme Island. The path leads you back onto the road you have already walked along twice and here you turn left again until the entrance gate of the YMCA centre.

Here you have to decide if you want to miss out the higher and longer route up Stott Park Heights, High Dam and Finsthwaite.

The low level route saves ¾ mile (1km) and 45 minutes. There is also 540ft (164m) less ascent. The route more or less follows the road, the first part being 'off road' on a permissive path. The last part of it is on the road, which is rather narrow and has quite a few blind bends, so walking this route needs much care and attention to the traffic. From here to Lakeside it is about 1½ miles (2.4 km) and does give you the opportunity of visiting Stott Park Bobbin Mill if you have an hour to spare. To do the low level route skip to the next box. The high level route is 2¼ miles (3.4 km) and involves a total ascent of 640 ft (195m).

So, taking the high level route, across the road you will see a gate in the wall. Pass through and strike upwards on the path that traverses the slope as it gradually ascends towards the top of Stott Park Heights. Ignore a left turn to go through a gate and upwards, eventually passing through an old wall and across a beck before climbing up a

Looking north up Windermere from Stott Park Heights.

rather steep and narrow path, which zigzags upwards. The path is not very obvious but has been lined with logs and branches and you will find occasional steps. It passes through another dilapidated wall where you bear left and follow the wall upwards. After 50 yards, at an orienteering post if it's still there, turn sharp right and ascend towards the summit. Just before approaching an oak tree, look out for a small path leading off to the left to the rocky outcrop of Stott Park Heights. (30)

You will find a seat at the summit where you can enjoy the views. Return down to the path and turn left, passing the oak tree, to follow the path which circumnavigates the outcrop in an anti-clockwise direction as it drops gradually down. The path eventually crosses a beck and then starts to ascend again towards High Dam reservoir, bearing right at a fork. You go through a gate and pass close to the water in the reservoir. (29)

If you wish you could walk all the way round in an anti-clockwise

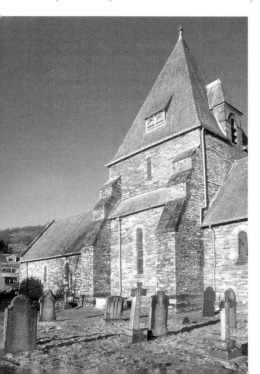

direction; it takes about 20 minutes. On a pleasant day and if you have the time it's well worth the small detour. From the dam back to Lakeside and the end of this section takes about 35–45 minutes.

Eventually you come to the dam and a path heads down beside the beck that leads to a smaller dam. Pass through a gate and then take the smaller path leading off to the right, not the wider path leading to the left. Carry on down on this rugged section and

St Peter's Church, Finsthwaite.

keep the beck on your right. Cross over the footbridge on your right after the rocky section of path and stride across the field, bearing slightly left and down across the slope. Waymarkers point you towards Finsthwaite which you soon reach, squeezing through a gap-stile to pass between some cottages. (28)

Bear right on the road and then first left towards the church. (27)

Go past the church and through the gate. Follow the path across two fields towards the trees and a stile into the cover of Great Knott Wood. Then follow the track down until it emerges onto the road again.

Turn right and, taking care, walk the short distance to Lakeside, where a launch or steamer will take you up the lake to Bowness or Ambleside-Waterhead. (26)

Low level route

This shortens the walk by ¾ mile (1 km) and about 45 minutes. The ascent will also be 540 ft (164m) less.

From the entrance to the YMCA, cross the road and walk along the road facing the oncoming traffic for about 200 yards. You will find a permissive path on your right which follows the boundary, with the road just over on your left. After about 500 yards the path crosses the road to the other side and the permissive path continues, with the road now over the boundary on your right for about the same distance, until you come to High Stott Park. You will now have to walk along the road to Lakeside and the road can be busy so keep well to the right-hand side and in single file; this is assuming there will be more than one person in the party. You soon pass Stott Park Bobbin Mill and it's worth a quick look even if you don't decide to stop.

Carry on along the road, still taking care, until you arrive at Lakeside where you can catch a steamer or launch back to Ambleside-Waterhead or Bowness.

Fell Foot to Lindeth Lane

7¾ miles (12.5 km),
approximately 3 hours 15 minutes
Total ascent 1483 ft (452m)

The start of the eastern section assumes you have found your way to the National Trust's Fell Foot Park. You may have left your car here to collect later, or you could travel back down the lake by either bus or boat, but check the details first. It doesn't really matter but this is the route that follows the eastern side of Windermere back to Ambleside-Waterhead.

Leave Fell Foot and walk south (or right) along the A592 in the direction of Newby Bridge. Soon a road leads off to your left up Fell Foot Road to Bowland Bridge. Follow this uphill for about ¾ mile (1.2km); sadly, this is quite boring though you may enjoy some good views of the lake as you struggle upwards. Pass a car park on your right and after 50 yards you will find a kissing gate on your left. This path leads to Gummer's How, which you will reach after about 10 minutes. The final bit is quite a steep climb over the rocks up to the top. There are many paths but if you take the one that seems to be going up towards the cairn, which you will earlier have observed is at the right-hand side of the top, you will eventually arrive at the highest point on *Windermere: Walking around the Lake* (1025 ft/313m). (25)

Having enjoyed the views, if the weather is clement, carry on from the top with the lake down on your left and head off onto a path leading off slightly to the right, not the one going steeply down. Passing through a few trees the path starts to descend and soon you bear right and down to the rather boggy ground which is full of clumps of rushes – the green spiky things growing up through the poor, damp grass. Turn left at the tree here and walk along a boggy

Looking down on Lakeside from Gummer's How.

path, with the slope up to your left, and pass through a dilapidated stone wall. Carry on along this path through the bracken, passing a single, tall larch tree on your right, and then right at the next junction of paths. After a few minutes the path starts to descend down towards a plantation. Climb over the ladder stile, next to a field gate, into Blake Holme Plantation and follow the path as it wends its way through the trees. Burrow Beck will be down on your right-hand side and you will be crossing this further on, so don't be tempted to follow one of the paths leading off to the left.

This narrow and often indistinct path eventually emerges onto another much more obvious path, and here you turn right over the beck and then left to join another path which climbs gently upwards. Eventually it comes near to a deer fence and then soon after a stile next to a gate takes you over a wall and out of the plantation.

Carry on ahead and round an outcrop to follow the path downwards. Pass through a gate and walk through the pasture with the boundary on your left to another gate. Through this carry on towards the house you can see ahead. Go through the gate and follow the path to go

The reservoir on Birkets Allotment.

over a step-stile in the wall on your left. Pass through this gate and down a narrow path to emerge in the garden of the next house. Follow the stepping stones across the grass and pass the front of the house.

Having walked through the garden of Low Moor Farm and gone past the barn on your left carry straight on to go through the gate ahead, following the yellow waymarker. The grassy track gradually descends and soon you emerge into a pasture, which slopes down to your right. Go ahead and down to the field gate and stile in the wall. Over in this next field follow the path, which soon bears right and descends to pass over a beck. Follow the track up to the wall ahead and bear left down the track to pass through two field gates and out on to a lane. Turn left and follow the road uphill. Near to the top you pass Low Ludderburn House on your right, the house where Arthur Ransome lived. (24)

The summit soon arrives in sight and then descends with a bend or two to a junction. Do not take the first turning to Winster but the second on your right, Ghyll Head Road. You will have passed the entrance to High and Low Moor How farms on your left. Follow Ghyll Head Road and after about 400 yards take the turning on your right and pass over the cattle-grid next to the gate set back from the road.

This quiet lane passes through a deer-proof gate before passing a reservoir and dam on your left. (23)

The track descends and at the bottom carry straight on through the gate and upwards on the bridleway. The path is now quite rugged again and you follow this for about ¾ mile until it descends and passes the entrance to High House Farm. Take the left-hand path, not over the stile, to the gate. (22)

Walk up to the next gate and then follow the rather muddy path with the wall still on your right. Turn right and follow the path along the 'intake' between the stone walls and on to the A5074 Lyth Valley road at the bottom. Go across the road and turn right into the lane almost opposite. After about 25 yards find a stile on your left and follow the path upwards and through the outcrops, following the overhead power lines, before going through a gate. This leads you into a pasture and across it is another gate. Follow the path to the gate at the right-hand side of the house and then follow the path though the next pasture to the farm ahead. Bear left and pass through the buildings at Lindeth. (21)

Next, bear right along the lane. At the end turn left and on to Lindeth Lane. Follow this lane to the junction with the B5284 Bowness–Kendal road.

Approaching Lindeth from the south.

To exit to Bowness.

This exit is 1¼ miles (2 km) long, taking about 45 minutes.

At the crossroads go into Lickbarrow Road and walk up the gentle incline for about 250 yards, then bear left up a track to a high stile over a wall, next to a gate. Follow the track ahead and as you approach Brantfell Farm bear left to follow the indistinct path with the wall on your right. At the top go over the stile on your right, not the one ahead, and go down the slope through the bushes and then bear right again down the pasture. A few steps lead you into another pasture where you bear left. This path is at the right-hand side of the field. It emerges onto a track where you cross over and continue ahead and eventually drop down, with the lake and Bowness in sight, to pass the end of the Dales Way and into Brantfell Road down into the centre of Bowness. Go to the lake shore at Bowness Bay. Here you can take a bus, or steamer, back to Ambleside.

The start of the Dales Way, just above Bowness.

Lindeth Lane to Ambleside

8¾ miles (14 km),
approximately 4 hours 15 minutes
Total ascent 1471 ft (449m)

To enter from Bowness

This entry is 1¼ miles (2 km) long, taking about 45 minutes.

From Bowness Bay walk towards the centre of Bowness and turn right into St Martin's Place, the narrow road opposite St Martin's Church. At the junction with the Lyth Valley Road, cross over to go up Brantfell Road to the left of the Spinney restaurant. At the top go over a stile and climb up to pass the start, or end, of the Dales Way. Continue upwards to cross a track and follow the path up through the meadow, with the trees on your left. At the top of this field you will see six steps up on your right. Take the path a short distance up the field and then bear to the left through some trees and over the wall. Follow the indistinct path left close to the wall. Soon you will be on the track leading away from Brantfell Farm and this leads you through fields to Lickbarrow Road. Turn right to the crossroads and then left.

If you are carrying straight on with the walk, just turn right and follow the road uphill for about ¾ mile (1.2 km), taking care on this rather busy road where cars should only drive at 40 mph, but usually go faster. (20)

Having passed the Windermere Golf Club look out for the entrance to Cleabarrow on your left. Next to the entrance is a concessionary path, the entrance of which is in the wall. Follow this until it emerges back onto the road again and immediately take the lane on your left. This is the Dales Way which goes all the way from Bowness to Ilkley in Yorkshire. Follow this through two gates until it bears right and upwards.

If you are missing out the climb up to School Knott skip to the next description box.

To carry on with the climb up to School Knott, go up the path on your right and having passed through a clump of gorse bushes, where the path can be rather wet, continue on to a gate. Here the Dales Way path turns right but you carry on through the field gate until you come to a small tarn. Bear left here, pass through a gate and follow the path up to School Knott. (19)

From the top bear left downhill and toward a stile. Go through this and taking the right-hand path go downhill through the newly planted trees to the track at the bottom. (18)

To miss out the climb up to School Knott

This shortens the walk by ½ mile (0.8 km) and about 20 minutes. The ascent will also be 150 ft (45m) less.

Keep straight on. Pass through a gate and across a rather rough pasture on the track to another gate. Carry straight on along the lane and soon pass the house called Old Droomer. Pass through another gate and at the next gate the path down from School Knott joins.

Both routes continue from here.

Bear right and go through the gate. Carry on and at the road cross over and straight on, with the houses over on your right, and keep on bearing right until you come to the rather splendid house and garden at Gill. (17)

Having admired the garden, go left over the footbridge and follow the steps up to the railway line and, taking great care, cross over it. Follow the path to the next gate and then turn right and follow the path to the road. This is the A591 Windermere–Kendal road coming down from Alice Howe. (16)

Turn right and cross over the road to take the road opposite to The Common. Again take care crossing over since cars rush at you from both directions. Walk along this lane for about 200 yards and take the footpath through the gate on your left. This is a permissive path which leads you up to Orrest Head. As it enters the trees bear right and then over two footbridges before climbing up through the trees. The path bears right and soon you come to a gateway. Pass through and immediately go up through the stile on your left to follow the path, which sometimes can be overgrown, up to the top of Orrest Head where there are a number of seats for you to sit and take in the views. (13)

From here you can either exit to Windermere town, or continue on to Waterhead.

To exit to Windermere town

This exit is ¾ mile (1.2 km) long, taking about 20 minutes.

Facing the lake go down the steps ahead of you and down to a kissing gate. (14)

Turn right and, at the end of the fence, turn left to wander down through the trees while still keeping to the left. The path is obvious but you don't want to stray to the right too much. You will find a good track at the bottom of this short stretch through the trees. Follow this past the blacksmith's and in about ten minutes you will be down in Windermere village on the main road from Ambleside. (15)

The tourist information office is across the road and so is the station where you can catch a bus or a train. Ambleside-Waterhead to Windermere town, 5¼ miles/8.4 km

The path up to Orrest Head from Windermere town. The left-hand path was the projected route of the railway line to Ambleside.

To enter from Windermere town

This entry is ¾ mile (1.2 km) long, taking about 20 minutes.

The start is next to the Windermere Hotel and opposite the National Westminster Bank on the A591 Kendal to Ambleside road. It is just across the road from the tourist information office and the bus and railway stations. (15)

The signpost points to Orrest Head and you simply follow the well-made track upwards. Having passed the blacksmith's building after 50 yards turn right and follow the wall on your right and then the path up through the trees. Turn right at the top along the path and pass through the kissing gate to go up the steps to Orrest Head. (14)

Having stopped to enjoy the view, the path you now seek is to your right, as you face the lake, and soon it goes steeply down. This path can be quite slippery when it's wet, frosty or dry; in other words most of the time! So, to quote A. Wainwright: 'Watch where you put your feet'. Go over the wall stile and carry on down, following the path as it heads towards Causeway Farm, the white farmhouse ahead. Pass over a beck and then a wall stile next to the gate onto the road, The Causeway, and turn right. (12)

After 200 yards go up the stone steps over the wall at Near Orrest. The path keeps to the right-hand boundary and passes through a gate and across the short field to go over two successive stiles. In this next field head for the corner of the stone wall about 75 yards ahead. Go over the steps in the wall. Do not carry on following the greener grass, which you may think is the correct route. Over this stile follow the boundary on your right and over another stile and then in this field don't follow the wall but cut across the field and then look for

Looking north from the path down from Orrest Head towards Causeway Farm.

The view enjoyed by the residents of Holehird.

a stile over the wall on your right. Bear left and head towards the farm buildings ahead. Go through a gate and across the track to go into the field opposite. Turn left and follow the fence, with the farmhouse over on your left. (11)

The gardens of the Lakeside Horticultural Society at Holehird in winter.

In a few paces go through the gate on your left and across the track to the gate opposite. Turn right and walk through this small enclosure, then through the gate on your left out into the entrance track to the farm. Turn right and walk away from the farm. Soon you will have another view of Windermere along the length of the lake, and of the Langdale Pikes and the fells surrounding the dale in the distance. Below on your left is Holehird, the house, gardens and lake. (10)

Soon you come to a narrow lane, cross over and walk up to the barn workshop ahead and the stile on its right-hand side. Go over and soon you will pass by a magnificent beech tree where you can rest and enjoy a splendid view on a good day. (9)

Follow the path through the next two pastures until you go through a kissing gate and out onto the Kirkstone Pass road. Cross over, turn right and walk along, soon taking the permissive path which soon

The 'bank' barn at Townend showing the upside entry to the hay loft.

brings you out onto the roadside again. As the road starts to drop downwards go through the kissing gate on your left, next to a field gate and bus stop. Follow the path down this pasture, through the gate at the bottom and over the two footbridges. Climb up the path which, at the top, emerges onto the road running up through Troutbeck village. Turn right and walk up the road and after about 200 yards you will come to a junction. On your left is Townend, a National Trust property, and a bank barn on your right. (8)

Carry straight on and look for an ascending path on your left, between two properties. This narrow path bends to the left and soon you will emerge at the top into Robin Lane. Turn left and follow the lane upwards for about 10 minutes, passing two tracks which lead off down to your left. Opposite the second one a stile in the wall leads to a pillar, which you will see above on your right-hand side. (7)

Soon you will come to the end of Robin Lane. A track leads off to your right up to The Hundreds, but you pass through the kissing gate next to the gate leading to Ambleside, Skelghyll and Jenkin(s) Crag. (6) and (2)

The pillar above Robin Lane between Troutbeck and Skelghyll.

The track, right, to The Hundreds on the easterly slopes of Wansfell.

This gently wends its way downwards until you emerge through another kissing gate onto a narrow lane. Turn right over the cattle-grid and follow the lane up to High Skelghyll Farm. (5)

Pass through the farm buildings. A gate leads you onto a path that soon brings you into Skelghyll Woods. (4) and (1)

As the path goes more steeply downwards you will notice the entrance to Jenkin Crag on your left, which you may wish to visit and to enjoy the view. (3)

Continue following the rugged path and after a particularly steep and uneven section. After the bridge, the path bends to the right and becomes more level. After a few paces look for a path down on your left. (*If you are going back to Ambleside carry straight on. The route is described below.*) This takes you down through the woods and over a ladder stile into a pasture. Walk across to the stile opposite and follow the path, which is quite rugged, back down to the main Ambleside–Windermere road. Across the road is Waterhead and the end of your walk.

The drove road from Ambleside to Troutbeck where, up till the mid-1800s, stock would be driven to markets in the south.

If you are going back to Ambleside carry on along the path and eventually it passes out of the woods. In a few minutes you will be on a narrow lane leading downhill. Soon you will come to Fisherbeck car park. Your car may be here, or walk through to the main road. Turn right and walk into Ambleside.

This is the end of the anti-clockwise walk around Lake Windermere.

Additional Walks from the Routes

The route for the walk around the lake can also be used as the basis for several comparatively shorter walks, as follows.

Walk 1: Ambleside/Waterhead and return via Skelghyll and the Low Wood Hotel.

2¾ miles (4.5 km). 1½–2 hours

The start is opposite the pier head at Waterhead, next to the bus stop on the main Ambleside–Windermere road. Across the road and to your right is the Waterhead Hotel and adjacent is the Lake House Hotel. Follow the sign to Jenkin Crag which takes you up a steep, rocky path and over a stile into a pasture. At the far side of the pasture there is a ladder stile over into Skelghyll Woods. The path ascends upwards through the trees, so you ignore a path descending to the right. Eventually it joins another path where you turn right.

Soon the track bears left and rises steeply and it's rough underfoot; so tread carefully, especially in wet conditions. Cross over Stencher Beck by the bridge and either take the left-hand bend, a gentler ascent, or carry straight on upwards. After another short, steep stretch of track the path becomes less steep.

This track used to be the 'drove road' from Ambleside to Troutbeck and then up the Garburn Road into Kentmere. From there it climbed over into Longsleddale, then south down the valley and eventually into the Lune Valley. Up until the middle of the nineteenth century, in fact until the coming of railways, cattle and sheep would be driven along drove

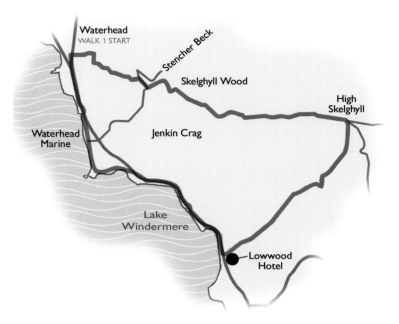

roads to the markets in the big cities and towns further south. So use your imagination and you will see hundreds of cattle and up to 2000 sheep being driven along this track by the drovers who would be on foot, not on horseback like the cowboys in the United States.

Look out on your right-hand side for the silver National Trust sign indicating 'Jenkin's Crag' on your right, over the wall. You will notice this time it has an apostrophe 's'.

Sometimes Jenkin Crag is also known as 'Jenkin's Crag', 'Jenkins Crag' or 'Jenkyn's Crag'. You may notice signs with all these spellings but it's the placement of the apostrophes which intrigues me. However I've used The Ordnance Survey spelling, which is no guarantee that it's the correct one, but at least it's the name which most people will be accustomed to. Jenkin by the way is the local dialect name for John. I'm afraid I don't know who Jenkin was. I think he must have been a farmer, or landowner, since there is a field directly below the crag next to the road between The Low Wood Hotel and Waterhead called Jenkin Field. For all I know he could indeed have been a Welshman, since Jenkin is a popular Welsh surname. Also we mustn't forget that the Welsh are more related to the Ancient British than the English and that the Ancient British lasted here in the Lake District longer than in the rest of England. That's why the old county of Cumberland gained its name; 'the land of the Cumri' and now we have a County of Cumbria. The Welsh for Wales is of course 'cymru', pronounced 'cumry'.

It's well worth a minute of two, or even longer, to go to the outcrop and look out over Windermere towards Wray on the far shore, the Coniston Fells further in the distance and, over to the right, the Langdale Pikes and other central fells.

Take note of the rock here. It is of the 'Borrowdale Volcanic Group' or 'BVG' as it's more commonly known and it's a good example, I believe, of what is known as 'pyroclastic flow' consisting of lumps (clasts) of rock thrown up from more than one source. It's been worn down by all the boots of those who visit this spot but away from the main viewpoints you can see the clasts more readily.

Looking west across Windermere from Jenkin Crag.

Returning to the track, turn right and continue the gradual climb upwards until the path is less steep and levels out.

The rock below you is limestone, a specific limestone known as 'Coniston Limestone', a narrow band of siltstone no more than a mile wide which stretches from Millom, on the coast near Barrow, to Shap passing across the northern reaches of Windermere. It overlays the BVG and is on the boundary of that rock and the softer Stockdale Shales of the Silurian period. This is why the topography to the south is gentler and less imposing than the fells to the north. The rocks have worn down more readily than the tougher volcanics. I'm no geologist but have been fascinated to find out about this particular 'unconformity', as I believe it's known, and anyone can see that the landscape is less rugged now.

Soon you leave the woods and the track 'contours' round to High Skelghyll Farm, with good views away on your right and down below you, the Low Wood Hotel, where you will be a little later in the walk.

I'm not sure of the derivation of Skelghyll but I do know that on Thomas Jeffrys' map of 1770 it is spelled 'Skel Gill' and it would seem that the 'ghyll' spelling has only become common since William Wordsworth started to spell it that way early in the nineteenth century.

As you walk down hill away from Skelghyll farm, take the grassy path off to the right, onto the hillside. It is to be found about 50 yards before you reach a cattle-grid, so if you come to a cattle-grid turn round, you have gone too far! Follow this path down the steeply sloping meadows and over a few stiles and descend towards the lake and the Low Wood Hotel.

The Low Wood Hotel is now very highly rated but it was originally a simple inn. In 1844 a meeting was held here to protest about the plans to bring the railway from Windermere to Ambleside, and even on to Keswick over Dunmail Raise. Amongst the local notables present was William Wordsworth, the most well-known personality, having just been appointed

The Lowwood Hotel, nestling beside the lake, seen from the path near to Skelghyll.

Poet Laureate. He wrote two very critical letters, including specially written sonnets to the Morning Post, *later incorporated into the* Daily Telegraph, *and which brought the topic into the public domain. His main argument was that it would spoil the nature of the Lake District but I suspect a darker motive was behind his protest. The campaign won, of course, but later Wordsworth bought shares in the line, despite his complaint that it was bringing common folk to 'assault' his treasured Lake District. Another example of the profound effect the poet had on the Lake District. You pass the hotel on your way by road from Windermere-Bowness to Ambleside; indeed you may even be staying here at this very well-appointed hotel.*

There's a café here should you feel like a reviving drink. Cross over the road and turn right and walk back towards Waterhead with the lake on your left over the wall. After a couple of bends look for a gate on the left leading you into the field owned by the National Trust. Go down to the shoreline at Holme Crag and follow the water's edge. You pass a boathouse and, as the field narrows, you emerge back onto the road through a gap in the wall at Waterhead Marine. It's now just a few strides back to Waterhead and the start of the walk.

Walk 2: Windermere town and return via Alice Howe.

1¾ miles (2.4 km). 1–1 ¼ hours

The start is just across the road from the tourist information office and the bus and railway stations and next to the Windermere Hotel. Opposite is the National Westminster Bank on the A591 Kendal to Ambleside road.

> The Windermere Hotel is one of the oldest buildings in the village of Windermere. It was opened in 1847, the same year that the railway came to Windermere, which at the time was called Birthwaite. From here horse-drawn coaches took visitors to Bowness, Ambleside and other parts.

The signpost points to Orrest Head and you simply follow the well-made track upwards as it twists and turns rather sharply.

The view from Orrest Head looking north-east to Troutbeck and its surrounding fells

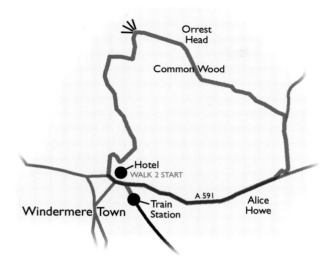

After a few yards up the track the path leading off to the left is the designated route of the railway line from Windermere to Ambleside that William Wordsworth ensured was never constructed.

After about 15 minutes you arrive at the blacksmith's. You will see some fine examples of Steve's work if you spare a minute or two – you may even be tempted into buying or commissioning a piece of his work. Just past here is a good place to view the lake, and after another 50 yards turn right and follow the wall on your right and then up through the trees. Turn right at the top along the path – seats to rest here – and then pass through the kissing gate to go up the steps to Orrest Head.

It was to Orrest Head that Alfred Wainwright came on his first, memorable, visit to the Lakes whilst on a day out by train from Blackburn. He was, of course, instantly captivated and

Enjoying the view of the lake from Orrest Head, showing the diorama.

spent most of the rest of his life enjoying hundreds of days out on the Lakeland fells and in the dales, capturing the various routes in pen and ink to the delight of millions. The name comes from the old Norse Orrusta *meaning 'a battle' so I assume this is the site of a battle early in the tenth century between the invading Norsemen and the 'English' who were descendants of the Anglo Saxon settlers. The outcrops of stone here are all Silurian Slate, which is the geological name of the underlying rock you will encounter during the whole of the walk. You may have read the stone tablet next to the kissing gate below that the widow and daughter of Arthur Heywood gave Orrest Head to the people of Windermere for public use in 1902.*

When you have enjoyed a rest, probably on one of the many seats here, and have taken in the panoramic view (explained on the diorama just below the top), stand facing the lake and take the grassy path on your left, which descends gently in a southerly direction to a stone wall. Turn left and follow the path, which may be overgrown by bracken in summer, down to a stile and onto a track. Turn right through the gateway and into the shelter of the trees in Common Wood. The path meanders and undulates through the wood until you pass through a wall where you turn left, downhill. After a few strides you pass through a collapsed wall; you may find that the path is not obvious but if you go straight down you will soon pick it up. The path then bears right and levels off and you go over a couple of footbridges before rising up slightly and then down again, bearing left. Go through a gate and into a field and at the far side there is another gate onto a lane. Turn right and walk along the lane to the main Windermere–Kendal road. You have to cross over here and this can be tricky with traffic coming at you quickly over the hill to your right.

This hill is known as Alice Howe and is marked as such on the OS map, but Thomas Jeffrys, the eighteenth-century cartographer, details it as 'Alliss Holme'. Who Alliss or Alice was I don't know but 'howe' is from the Old Norse haugr – 'mound or knoll', whereas 'holme' is what the islands of Windermere are usually called. So I can only assume Mr Jeffrys was either confused or deaf!

Follow the road past Alice Howe Farm and back down to Windermere town. You may notice you are sharing the footpath with cyclists, so take care since it's doubtful that many will have purchased a bell. I have one on my bike but it seems as though most cyclists cannot afford the extra £5 after they have purchased their £800 bike!

Soon you will be back near the stations, both railway and bus.

The original station is now incorporated into Booths Supermarket and retains the superb porte-cochère *station entrance. If you have time to spare why not pop into Booths; they have a good range of delicious food, as much as possible sourced locally. Or visit the nearby Lakeland main store to buy one of those kitchen gadgets you just can't live without.*

Walk 3: Fell Foot Brow and return via Gummer's How and Ludderburn Park.

3¾miles (6km). 2–2½ hours.

The start of this walk is to be found at the top of Fell Foot Brow, just off the Newby Bridge–Windermere Road (A592), opposite Fell Foot Park. Park your car at the car park almost at the top of Fell Foot Brow, on the right. Stride a few yards uphill on the road to the gate on your left. This path leads to Gummer's How, which you will reach after about 10 minutes. The final bit is quite a steep climb, or scramble, over the rocky outcrops up to the top. There are many paths but if you take the one that seems to be going up towards the cairn, which you will earlier have observed is at the right-hand side of the top, you will eventually arrive at the highest hill surrounding Lake Windermere (1025ft/313m). You may think Wansfell, near to Ambleside, is higher and you are right but it isn't just above the lake, as is Gummer's How.

The cairn on Gummer's How and the valley below wreathed in mist.

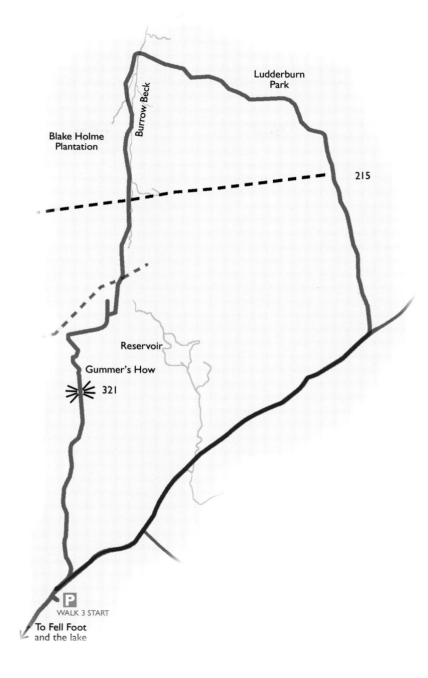

Ludderburn
Park

Blake Holme
Plantation

Burrow Beck

215

Reservoir

Gummer's How

321

P
WALK 3 START

To Fell Foot
and the lake

Hopefully you will appreciate splendid views of the Lakeland Fells to the north and west. You may also enjoy more good views of the eastern fells: the Howgills, the Pennines, Ingleborough and, towards the southeast, the relatively low range of the Bowland Fells, inland from Lancaster, and the distinctive tower at the motorway services just south of Lancaster. Also you should be able to see almost the whole length of the lake from a different perspective. You may find it hard to believe that only 200 years ago most of the trees you see around the lake would not have been there, most of the surrounding land being rough grassland grazed bare by sheep. The name of this hill is derived from the Old English and means 'a hill owned by a man called Godmund.' To the south you may also be able to see the expanse of Morecambe Bay and the Kent estuary at Arnside. The River Kent passes through Kendal. To the south-west you may be able to see the tower on Hoad Hill, a lighthouse-like structure overlooking Ulverston. It was constructed to commemorate Sir John Barrow, who was born in Ulverston in 1764. It is in the style of a former Eddystone Lighthouse and celebrates Sir John's career as the Second Secretary to the Admiralty. He is best remembered for his support of the exploration of the Arctic and the Northwest Passage.

Having enjoyed the views, if the weather is clement, carry on from the top, heading north with the lake down on your left, and find a path leading off slightly to the right of the cairn (not the one going steeply down on the right). It passes through a few trees and then the path starts to descend through the bracken. Soon your bear right at a junction of paths and down to the rather boggy ground which is full of clumps of rushes – the green spiky things growing up through the poor, damp grass. Turn left at the tree here and walk along a boggy path, with the slope up to your left, and soon pass through a dilapidated stone wall. Carry on along this path through the bracken, passing a single, tall larch tree on your right and then right at the next junction of paths. After a few minutes the path starts to descend down towards a plantation. Climb over the ladder stile, next to a field gate, into Blake Holme Plantation and follow the path as it wends its way through the trees. Burrow Beck will be down on your right-hand side. You will be crossing this further on, so don't be tempted to follow one of the paths leading off to the left

The narrow path eventually brings you out on to a wider path. Turn right here and having walked over Burrow Beck follow the track straight on and upward towards Ludderburn Park. Simply follow this path until it nears a wall and then levels off, where it can be quite boggy. The path passes through the trees on a relatively good path until it emerges out onto the road, where you turn right and walk about one mile (1¾ kms) back to your car. Keep to the right, facing the oncoming traffic.

Walk 4: Lakeside and return via High Dam reservoir and Stott Park Heights.

4½ miles (7.2 km). 2½–3 hours.

Lakeside is a product of the Victorian tourist boom, being created by the link of the railway with the lake steamers. Tourists would travel by coach and horse, later by tram, from Blackpool to Fleetwood and then sail across Morecambe Bay to Barrow from where they would take a train to Lakeside. From Lakeside they would sail up to Waterhead and back and then return to Blackpool. Quite a long day out and no doubt an exciting one for the Lancashire mill workers who formed the bulk of the visitors. Here there is a splendid aquarium, and the steam train journey to Haverthwaite and back is quite an experience too. At Lakeside there is good provision for refreshments and a comfort break before you start your walk. There isn't anywhere else until the end of the day.

So to start the walk leave the car park and go past the entrance to the Lakeside Hotel and on to the Newby Bridge–Hawkshead road.

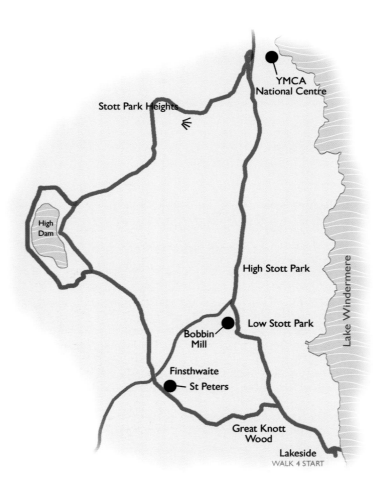

Turn right and walk along the road, taking care to watch out for traffic. After about 300 yards, or about 5 minutes, there is a footpath on the left-hand side of the road going up through trees and leading to Finsthwaite. Cross over, taking care at this rather sharp bend in the road, and climb up the track through Great Knott Wood. Soon you are at the top and the path emerges into a field, where you head across in the direction of the church. After walking through two fields you will go through a gate and find yourself on another track, which passes the church.

The present church of St Peter, built in 1874, replaces a much older chapel. There is an interesting grave in the churchyard. It is a grave with a cross next to a 'table grave' on the opposite side of the church to the porch. This is the resting place of Clementina Johannes Sobiesky Douglass who died on 16 May 1771 and who, it is suggested, was an illegitimate daughter of Prince Charles Edward Stuart (Bonnie Prince Charlie). Why she lived and died here is a matter of conjecture. The facts do seem to have a semblance of truth since Prince Charles' mother was named Maria Clementina and was the granddaughter of King John Sobieski of Poland. Douglas was the family name of Charles. It is an intriguing mystery and if you want to follow it up there is a booklet published by the Cumberland & Westmorland Antiquarian & Archaeological Society entitled The Finsthwaite Princess: the making of a myth *written by Janet D. Martin. Just as a matter of interest, in another St Peter's, the Basilica of St. Peter in Rome, there is an enormous monument above the tomb of Maria Clementina Sobieski, the wife of James Stuart, the Old Pretender. It reaches about 25 feet high and is set between two marble columns, quite near the entrance. Could there be a greater contrast between the memorials to two such similarly named women?*

Leaving the church go straight up the lane opposite into the centre of the village, next to the house with the interesting balcony.

This small hamlet is an ancient place named after a man called Finn, a Norseman who had a farmstead in the clearing

101

here – 'thwaite' being the Norse for 'clearing'. You will notice that the village is still surrounded by trees and is probably not a lot different in its setting, apart from the houses here, than it was a thousand years ago.

At the junction turn right and after a few yards take the indicated path on your left, up past a few cottages and over a stile into a field. You should see yellow waymarkers here and you follow these, but essentially you are going straight on to ascend through the first field and into the next heading, for the trees. You cross over a beck and turn left to wend your way gradually upward, keeping the beck on your left. In a few minutes, after a stiff ascent, you will come to Low Dam reservoir, the small, subsidiary reservoir below the much larger reservoir just above. The beck you've walked alongside, or at least near to, comes down from this. Carry on upwards to a bigger dam, High Dam (567ft/173m), and the delightful reservoir which, I believe, is one of the Lake District's hidden gems, even though it is man made.

Low Dam reservoir and, at the far side, the dam of its big sister.

The Coniston Fells seen from the path leading up to Stott Park Heights.

You can't help but notice that the High Dam reservoir holds a considerable amount of water and it would certainly have been sufficient to power Stott Park Bobbin Mill, situated lower down near the lake and which you will pass, or even visit, later on in the walk.

Walk across the dam and follow the footpath, with the water down on your right. You will come across a junction of paths, so take the path to the right indicated by a white arrow. This is a permissive path. Soon a conveniently situated seat affords a splendid place for a rest. At the end of the circuit of the reservoir you pass through a gateway and soon bear left on the track to pass though a kissing gate.

Ahead you will soon see a massive outcrop and this is Stott Park Heights, your next objective. At the bottom cross over the beck, bear left and follow the path as it wends its way clockwise around the outcrop, upwards through holly trees, Scots pines and others. Soon you achieve a levelling off of the path, with views towards the Coniston Fells and those north of the lake. So look out for a path leading off to the right. This brings you out onto the top of the outcrop which is covered in heather. Search out a path which takes you to the viewpoint and seat. This crosses the rocks which are

103

Looking north from Stott Park Heights.

aligned in ridges running across the path, north–south, and can be a bit tricky to negotiate.

Soon you will be at the viewpoint. The name Stott Park Heights suggests something majestic but even though it is only 636ft/193m above sea level it is, I'm sure you will agree, a good place to admire the surrounding fells and the lake.

> *You will find a bench here which is a good place to have a coffee or lunch break, or just a few minutes' rest, during which period you may see and undoubtedly hear one or two supersonic jets scream past below you. Look across Windermere and see Blake Holme Island or 'Wild Cat Island', as it is known in Arthur Ransome's Swallows and Amazons. This is just to your left against the opposite shore and, up above, Gummer's How is just to your right by about 10 degrees.*

Leaving the top go to the left down the steep slope and find the narrow path on which you ascended earlier. This goes down to your right, at first steeply. You will arrive at a dilapidated wall and, perhaps, an orienteering post if it's still there. Turn left and down with the wall on your right. After 50 yards go through a break in the wall and down steeply, following the rather rugged and steeply descending path which is not easy to pick out. It's been lined with fallen branches and there are occasional steps. It zigzags two or three times before approaching a beck, which will be on your left as you go down the slope. Stride over and through another dilapidated wall. The descent becomes more gradual and in a few minutes you will pass through a gate where you continue ahead and soon find you have descended back down to the road you left earlier to climb up through the woods to Finsthwaite.

Opposite is the YMCA centre, so turn left and walk along the road facing the oncoming traffic for about 200 yards. You will find a permissive path on your right which follows the boundary, with the road just over on your left. After about 500 yards the path crosses the road to the other side and the permissive path continues with the road now over the boundary on your right for about the same distance, until you come to High Stott Park. You will now have to walk along the road back to Lakeside, and it can be busy so keep well to the right-hand side and in single file; this is assuming there will be more than one person in the party. You soon pass Stott Park Bobbin Mill and it's worth a quick look even if you don't decide to stop.

Even if you haven't time to stop it's really well worthwhile coming back another time if you are interested in industrial and social history. It was just one of many mills in this area which produced bobbins for the cotton mills further south in Lancashire. Trees growing in the surrounding woods were specially coppiced to produce the right sort of timber for these bobbins, as well as to produce charcoal. The bark was also often used in the process of tanning. The mill operated from 1835 until 1971. In 1983 English Heritage purchased the remains and it has become a 'living museum', where you can see how a typical mill of this type operated. The original steam engine is still in situ *and can be seen working, although the machinery is now powered by electricity*

From here it's a short walk back to Lakeside but you are still following the road with its many blind bends.

Walk 5: The Ferry House and return via Claife Heights.

5¼ miles (8.4 km). 3–3½ hours.

If you are starting the day on the eastern shore of Windermere you will have to make your way to the car ferry, 15 minutes walk south from Bowness, and cross over to the to the shore at Ferry House. In summer you can also take a launch from Bowness Bay to the same place; this saves the ¾ mile walk to Ferry Nab.

Make your way from the landing stage along the road to the junction. If you arriving at the start from the western side you can park a car at the National Trust car park at Ash Landing. A path takes you toward the car ferry and the start of the walk.

Look for the footpath going up through the trees and follow this footpath up the rather steep slope following the white route as indicated. However, to be sure you follow the correct route I will describe it. Climb up the track until soon you come to an old ruin.

This is a 'viewing station' constructed in the late eighteenth century by one of the Curwens of Belle Isle for the use of those of a 'romantic persuasion' who toured the Lake District taking in the 'breathtaking and sometimes frightening views'. There is an explanation on a couple of boards attached to the walls. Various writers of tour guides had equally varying opinions. Thomas West, author of A Guide to the Lakes *held it in high regard, whilst the Frenchman, Louis Simond, author of* A journal of a tour and residence in Great Britain *during 1810 and 1811, wrote; ... Affords no favourable specimen of proprietor's taste ... Simond was married to an Englishwoman, the niece of John Wilkes, the great eighteenth-century journalist and politician.*

From here climb up the path which, as you ascend, provides good views of Belle Isle and across the lake to Bowness. The path passes through a rocky outcrop and is quite steep in parts then levels out

The ruins of the 'Viewing Station'.

somewhat as it traverses the slope, often scrambling over another set of rocky outcrops and more or less following the contour line of Mitchell Knotts.

Eventually you walk through trees and pass through a kissing gate onto a bridleway. Turn left and walk to the next junction. Here, turn right at the finger post, painted white at the top with a number 3 on it and on which should be affixed a map outlining the white route. The route follows quite a good track between stone walls on either side of which are pastures and soon you pass a small tarn, from the Old Scandinavian meaning a 'tear', an apt description I always feel.

Follow this path as it gently undulates along the crest of Claife Heights, though there is one short steep descent, followed by a similar ascent. At 'Junction 4' don't turn left but carry straight on with an old wall on your right and a gap in the wall leads to Low Pate Crag.

You may wish to stop a while and go to the lookout where you will have a splendid view up and down the lake and, directly below where you stand, of Belle Isle and Bowness. Brant Fell, School Knot and Orrest Head are the three hills you can spot from left to right behind Bowness.

The Lake and Bowness from Mitchell Knotts.

Return to the path, turn right and follow the undulating path, soon passing right through the wall when the path offers more good views of the lake, and across to the eastern route and the distant Howgill Fells. This path takes you along the part of Claife Heights known as The Heald for about a mile before crossing a ford, when you follow the track for about 250 yards to the well paved bridleway, which was the packhorse route between Hawkshead and the lake. Here turn right, downhill, to Belle Grange, where you turn right onto the lake side route.

The path is quite uneven for about a mile but you may encounter a car and, almost certainly, cyclists. Passing through a gate/cattle-grid the surface improves and you will be closer to the lake.

Directly opposite is Windermere's largest island, Belle Isle, which is about 1000 yards (1 kilometre) in length. There are also three adjacent small islands just off the shore. The bigger island to the north is Thompson's Holme and the other two are known as Lilies of the Valley. Belle Isle was originally called 'Langholme' – 'long island' – but was purchased by a John English who built the round house in 1774, which you may glimpse hiding amongst the trees. Isabel Curwen bought it prior to her marriage to John Christian, who subsequently

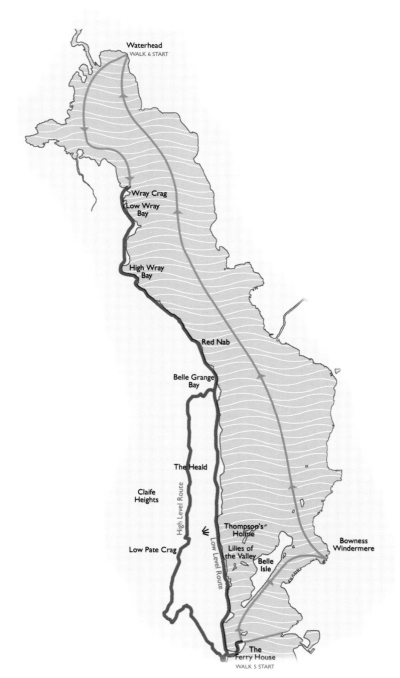

Waterhead
WALK 6 START

Wray Crag
Low Wray Bay

High Wray Bay

Red Nab

Belle Grange Bay

The Heald

Claife Heights

High Level Route

Low Level Route

Low Pate Crag

Thompson's Holme

Lilies of the Valley

Belle Isle

Bowness Windermere

The Ferry House
WALK 5 START

> *took the name Curwen. Up on your right is Heald Wood on the slopes of Claife Heights. 'Claife' comes from the Old Norse and means 'steep hillside up which there is a path '.*

This is good place to take a rest but be careful where you sit. This is a favourite place for Canada geese and other waterfowl and they don't care where they deposit their mess. Follow the lane until it passes quite close to the water at Mitchell Wyke

> *As you can see, it is a popular place to moor boats, being sheltered by the nab on which Ferry House is built. It is also, incidentally, the place where I first remember coming to Windermere when I was about 15 years old. I stayed overnight on a boat by the name of* Marshall Soult, *just one of many motor cruisers ('The Little Ships', as they became known) which answered the call to rescue British troops from the shores of France at Dunkirk in 1940. I must have enjoyed that first visit since I keep coming back to Windermere and the Lakes.*

After a few more paces you are at the junction you were at the beginning of your walk and left takes you to the car ferry or launch back to Bowness.

The sheltered west of the lake, with Belle Isle on the right, the Lillies of the Valley in the near distance and the ripple peaks of Froswick, Ill Bell and Yoke in the distance, just to the right of centre.

Walk 6: Ambleside-Waterhead and return via the eastern path of Windermere and a launch and a steamer.

3½ miles (5.6 km). 2 hours walking plus about 1 hour and 10 minutes on the water.

This is quite an interesting circular outing, which can also be started from Bowness. The walk is done in conjunction with the Windermere steamship company so just order a 'walkers ticket' and off you go. Sadly this service only operates during the summer months, so do check before you make a decision. The launch to take is the one to Brockhole, the Lake District National Park Visitor Centre. It usually runs from Easter to the end of October once every hour from about 9.45am.

This walk also covers the latter part of Walk 5, and uses the same map (see page 109). If you would like to make it a little bit more rigorous turn to page 64 and take the high level route from Belle Grange to the Ferry House.

Start from the pier at Waterhead from where you take the launch to Low Wray Bay; this stop is by request so don't forget to mention you have a walker's ticket.

From the jetty at Low Wray Bay you follow the permissive path south through the trees, with the lake on your left. After climbing up a short, steep incline you climb over a stile. Wray Castle is just about visible up on your right and you may wish to climb up to have a look. You can't go in but you can walk around the outside area. Over the stile carry straight on and then drop down to the left to the lake shore and High Wray Bay. Follow the path along, with the lake down on your left. Pass through a gate onto a track and turn left past High Wray Bay. Having gone through two gates the path closely follows the lake shore to Red Nab.

From Red Nab the route follows a bridleway so you may well meet an occasional car or motor bike and almost certainly a number of cyclists.

Pass through a gate and follow the track to Belle Grange. You may wish to follow the high level route here as described on page 64. This adds an extra ¾ mile (1km). It also involves an ascent of 654 ft (199m) and takes about an hour longer. Otherwise carry on following this low level track, with one rise up and down all the way, passing off shore Thompson's Holme, the Lilies of the Valley and Belle Isle, the longer island further out from the shore. The grassy bank here is a pleasant place to sit if the waterfowl haven't fowled it before hand. Further on you pass by Mitchell Wyke, the sheltered bay full of boats, and at the junction turn left to the Ferry House where a launch will take you to Bowness.

At Bowness you transfer to the steamer to take you back to Waterhead. This is a journey of about 35 minutes.

On the other hand you can start this circular day out at Bowness, sail on the steamer to Waterhead and take the Brockhole launch to Low Wray Bay to commence the walk.